The Ultimate Pizza

The World's Favorite Pizza Recipes—
From Deep-Dish to Dessert

Pasquale Bruno, Jr.

CB
CONTEMPORARY
BOOKS
A TRIBUNE NEW MEDIA COMPANY

Library of Congress Cataloging-in-Publication Data

Bruno, Pasquale.
    The ultimate pizza : the world's favorite pizza recipes—from deep-dish to
dessert / Pasquale Bruno, Jr.
        p.   cm.
    Includes index.
    ISBN 0-8092-3349-5
    1. Pizza. 2. Cookery, International. I. Title.
TX770.P58B78 1995
641.8'24—dc20   95-31565
                                                                              CIP

Illustrations by Lana Mullen
Interior design by Nancy Freeborn

Copyright © 1995 by Pasquale Bruno, Jr.
All rights reserved
Published by Contemporary Books, Inc.
Two Prudential Plaza, Chicago, Illinois 60601-6790
Manufactured in the United States of America
International Standard Book Number: 0-8092-3349-5
10 9 8 7 6 5 4 3 2 1

To my daughters, Carol and Patricia, with love and affection,

and

To my wife, Gale, who through thick (crust) and thin (crust) has never failed

to answer the call "The pizza is ready."

CONTENTS

ACKNOWLEDGMENTS

Many people played a role in my pizza education, but my mother, who made pizza at least once a week, the best pizza you would ever want, was the best teacher of them all. A number of years passed before I could put into practice what she taught me, and it wasn't until then that I realized what a good pizzamaker she truly was.

She was a traditionalist through and through, however. It was pizza with either pepperoni or sausage—nothing more, nothing less. It wasn't until after I left home when I was eighteen and started traveling the world that I got beyond my pepperoni and sausage pizza days. It has been one great pizza ride ever since.

Along the way I learned a lot. I grew up in New York, so I knew about New York–style pizza, but in Boston's North End I got another look at great thin-crust pizza when I discovered Pizzeria Regina and many others.

When I moved to Chicago in the late '60s, I learned about Chicago deep-dish pizza from the late Ike Sewell, the father of deep-dish pizza. About the same time, the late Nick Perrino, the owner of Home Run Pizza, acquainted me with thin-crust pizza—Chicago-style. How wonderful it was and still is today.

Thanks go out to the thousands of people who have attended my seminars on pizza each year at the annual get-together of the National Association of Pizza Operators. I may have been the teacher, but I learned a lot from the questions asked.

Thanks to Gerry Durnell, the publisher of *Pizza Today* magazine, who for the past eleven years has given me the opportunity to write a monthly column on pizza, helping me to stretch my knowledge of the subject even further.

Thanks to the many pizzamakers—more names than I can mention here—that I have worked with in this country and abroad who have shared with me an idea, a technique, a story, a slice of pizza or two. The memories are great.

It was at Demarini's restaurant in Fish Creek, Wisconsin, that Vito Demarini, one of the best pizzaioli I have ever known, taught me and reminded me that the best pizza dough is the simplest, so I especially wish to thank him.

At Contemporary Books, I am grateful to Nancy Crossman.

Thank you, Christine Benton, for the care and attention that you have given to each of my recipes in every cookbook I have written. Your editorial skills (not to mention all of those yellow query slips) are something else.

INTRODUCTION: A SLICE OF HISTORY

The prediction is that by the end of this year pizza will push the hamburger out of its number-one spot as America's favorite food. Those of us in the business knew that it was just a matter of time—and for a lot of reasons. You can do only so much with a hamburger to create excitement day in and day out (but you sure have to admire Dave Thomas of Wendy's for creating a lot of "fun on a bun"). I mean, let's face it, we're talking about a piece of meat and a bun.

Pizza is another story altogether. Pizza comes in all shapes, thicknesses, and sizes. Pizza has panache. Pizza can be topped with just about any type of food, which keeps it not just tasty but interesting as well. Pizza knows no age limits; from the very young to the very old pizza is a food that everyone enjoys. *Pizza* is a word recognized around the world, so the product is clearly understood, and the appeal is universal. Pizza can be frozen and brought back to life almost as good as new (try that with a hamburger).

Pizza delivers well, tastes great cold (Want a great cure for a hangover? Cold pizza with cold milk works every time), and can be bought by the slice, the whole pie, or a whole bunch of pies.

Where did this monumental piece of food work come from? Is there someone special we should honor, some particular person (like Caesar Cardini, who created the Caesar salad in 1924) we can name as the creator of this fabulous food we call *pizza*? I'm afraid not. Pizza evolved over such a long period of time that it is impossible to trace its origins to any particular person or eating place (the hamburger, in its present form, can be traced back to an 1836 menu from Delmonico's restaurant in New York City).

Despite the mystery shrouding the origins of this humble pie, there is still plenty of pizza history to digest. Some of the historical information available to us is rooted in facts so solid that they stand alone. Other information has been (as sometimes happens in history) pieced together like a grand mosaic to form a complete picture of pizza's evolution. Still, as it goes in matters of food history, some of the stories about the origins of pizza are apocryphal.

For example, there is no foundation to support the idea that the word *pizza* derives from an Old Italian word meaning "a point." But if we look at the Italian word *pizzicare*, which means "to pinch" or "to pluck," as in plucking a pizza from the oven, we are getting closer to the origin of the word.

The question of when the tomato first appeared on pizza stirs hot debate among food historians. Everyone agrees (more or less) that the tomato (seeds actually) traveled from the lower

Andes, in an area that today covers parts of Ecuador, Peru, and Bolivia, to Spain in the 16th century. (The seeds from Peru bore small yellow tomatoes; hence the name *pomo d'oro* or *golden apple*.) Shortly thereafter, circa 1522, the tomato showed up in Italy—Naples to be exact (stay tuned; the pizza is on its way).

However, like most foods coming from the New World, the tomato was looked on with great suspicion (the Italian naturalist Pierandrea Mattioli in 1544 was the first to write about the tomato, describing it as *mala insana* or "unhealthy apple"). Used mostly as an ornamental plant, the tomato did not come into favor as a food until the middle of the 18th century, when it began to take hold of the Italian taste buds. Waverley Root writes in his book *Food* that "Italians were tomato pioneers in the kitchen as well as in the garden. The first cook to use it much as we do today was Francesco Leonardi, probably Roman-born, who worked his way up to the position of cook for Catherine II of Russia. His most [prolific] period fell between 1750 and 1788, a century before the Americans abandoned the practice of a three-hour stewing for this distrusted food."

Now that we have some dates and the tomato question settled, let's go back to the very beginning. The comparison between pizza and pita bread has not been lost on some food historians, who suggest that pizza has Arab origins. But the fact is that Cato (Roman statesman, soldier, and writer, 234–149 B.C.) writes about "flat rounds of dough dressed with olive oil, herbs and honey and baked on stones."

In 1840, Francesco de Bourcard, a Neapolitan food historian, said of pizza, "Pizza is a specialty of the Neapolitans and of the very city of Naples itself [the first known pizza shop was Port 'Alba in Naples. It opened in 1830 and is still open today]. If you want to know what a pizza is, take a piece of dough, roll it out, pummel it a bit with the flat of your hands, cover it with anything at all, moisten it with oil or lard, bake it in the oven and eat it."

With these dates as fact, we know that tomatoes were not an essential part of pizza—they might have been used on occasion but were not important at that point—until sometime after 1840.

As the 19th century was coming to a close, pizza—pizza baked in coal-fired ovens that reached temperatures upward of 750°F—became as important to Naples as Sophia Loren was some sixty years later. Pizza was being sold from stalls and eaten on the street with great relish from midday until the wee hours of the morning. Pizza became the first fast food known to man.

Pizza ascended to another plateau in 1889, when King Umberto I made a visit to Naples. At his side was Queen Margherita, who immediately wanted to try this food she had heard so much about. Now we get to the good stuff. The story goes that, of course, the queen wasn't going to a humble pizzeria, so the pizza was brought to whatever palazzo the royal couple was staying at (here we have the first pizza delivery). The pizza was delivered by Raffaele Esposito, owner of the famous pizzeria Pietro il Pizzaiolo. Esposito went with his wife, Donna Rosa, who was, in fact, the pizzamaker. They brought enough ingredients to make three kinds of pizza, and after sampling all three, Queen Margherita selected as her favorite the pizza made with tomatoes, mozzarella, and fresh basil. Obviously patriotism met good taste head-on, the pizza colors—red, white, and green—being the same as those of the Italian flag. Nevertheless, pizza Margherita is to this day one of the most popular pizzas sold in the United States as well as Italy.

Pizza was pretty much a food of Italy alone until the great wave of immigrants flooded American shores at the turn of the century. Bakeries and grocery stores sprang up in New York City's Little Italy neighborhood. A sideline of the bakeries was pizza. Pizza made with the same dough used for Italian bread was pressed into large rectangular pans and consisted simply of dough, tomato puree, oregano, basil, and grated Romano cheese. The mozzarella the Italian immigrants had found on these shores was much different from the softer, creamier mozzarella di bufala (made with the milk of the water buffalo) they were used to in Italy—and it was costly, too—so for a time the pizzamakers eschewed it. Gradually, however, mozzarella found its way onto what at that time must have been considered a specialty pizza.

In the first decade of the 20th century many of the pizzamakers toiling in these Italian bakeries decided it was time to get what they had come to this country for in the first place—a business and a better life for their families. Leaving the bakeries behind, they opened pizza parlors, establishments that sold pizzas—whole, by the slice, and to take home (pasta was on the menu too).

Food historians have conceded—only, I suspect, because it has been mentioned so often—that the first true pizzeria (not a bakery selling pizza) was opened in 1905 by Gennaro Lombardi on Spring Street in New York City. Others followed quickly. New York's Little Italy began to look a lot like a Little Naples in that regard. During the 1930s pizzerias sprouted up in profusion along the eastern seaboard. Pizza was fast becoming a food of note.

The real catalyst that moved the pizza business forward in this country, though, was the GIs returning from Italy after World War II. They remembered well the wonderful flavor of the pizza they had eaten in Italy, so pizza was swept along with the fast-food revolution that occurred in this country in the early '50s.

Chicago-style or deep-dish pizza (also called *pan pizza*) was a part of the great pizza boom that spread from the East Coast into the Midwest toward the end of the war. In 1943 Pizzeria Uno was opened in Chicago, followed shortly by Pizzeria Due, and they were an instant success.

I should point out that thin-crust pizza, similar to that being made in New York City, was already being sold in the Italian bakeries that lined Taylor Street—the Little Italy section of Chicago— in the early 1900s and later in small pizzerias around Chicago.

And so, as this century comes to a close and pizza has rolled around the globe, we have to admire how far it has come from those humble beginnings. The fact that we pummel it (did de Bourcard know what was coming?), stretch it, machine it, freeze it, microwave it, top it with anything and everything, and it still has a taste and appeal that people love, is grand testimony to the greatness of the food. What, can we imagine, will pizza be like in the year 2050? Send me a menu in care of Saint Peter.

Pasquale Bruno
Chicago, 1995

Chapter 1

ABOUT PIZZA DOUGH

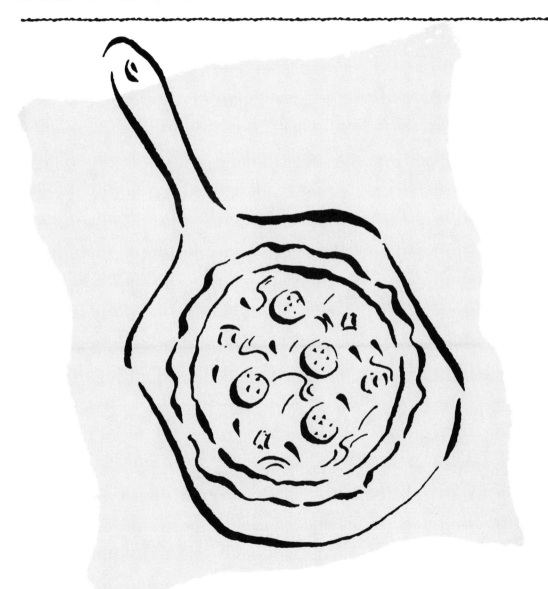

Dough for a pizza can be made with but four ingredients: flour, salt, yeast, and water. Those four ingredients, which are pretty much the same as those used for bread, perform certain functions and will make a decent dough, provided they are handled properly. Nevertheless, the struggle to produce the perfect pizza crust is never ending, so sugar or shortening, milk or olive oil, seasonings and dough additives can be mixed in. Then there are different kinds of flour such as whole-wheat, cornmeal, semolina . . . the list seems to grow daily.

Each of these variables will, of course, affect how the dough turns out, so it's important that the pizzamaker understand the function of each ingredient. Once you do, you'll understand how this simple yeast dough works and, most critically, what to do when things aren't going right. Knowing the following cause-and-effect relationships can help you become an expert pizzamaker, a first-rate *pizzaioli*.

HOW YEAST DOUGH WORKS

In its simplest form, pizza dough is flour mixed with water and yeast. But to understand what pizza dough is all about it is important to understand how those three ingredients work.

When flour and water are mixed together and kneaded the dough becomes elastic, since the protein in the flour absorbs the water, and gluten is developed. The addition of yeast—a leavening agent—is the critical ingredient in the making of dough. Yeast grows and splits the natural sugars present in the flour to form carbon dioxide. It is the carbon dioxide—a gas—trapped within the gluten structure that causes the dough to rise.

PRIMARY FUNCTIONS OF DOUGH INGREDIENTS

Flour
- Acts as a binding agent
- Acts as an absorption agent
- Provides structure
- Affects the quality of taste
- Provides nutrition

Water

◆ Aids in the dissolving of yeast and the dispersion of other ingredients

◆ Acts as a binding agent

◆ Unites the protein in the flour, the protein being responsible for gluten development (see "Flour" section)

Yeast

◆ Acts as a fermentation agent, providing the dough with volume (In conjunction with water and flour, yeast produces carbon dioxide through fermentation. As the carbon dioxide gas is produced, the dough rises.)

◆ Affects flavor

Salt

◆ Stabilizes fermentation (controls yeast growth)

◆ Affects flavor

◆ Strengthens gluten

◆ Affects texture and grain of the dough

Shortenings and Oils

◆ Enhance the keeping qualities of the dough

◆ Affect flavor

◆ Aid elasticity of dough

◆ Increase tenderness

Sugar

◆ Increases fermentation tolerance (extends the life of the yeast)

◆ Affects texture and grain

◆ Tenderizes

◆ Affects flavor

◆ Aids in browning

Milk and Milk Solids

- Add nutritional value
- Affect flavor
- Increase tenderness

Dough Additives

- Improve elasticity
- Bulk up protein content of flour

DOUGH TROUBLESHOOTING

Problem: Dough is bucky and hard to stretch after kneading.

Causes: Not enough water in basic recipe.
  Gluten content of the flour may be too high.
  Dough formula needs a lubricant (oil or shortening).
  Dough has not been given enough rising time.

Problem: Dough has poor grain and texture.

Causes: Flour is poor quality.
  Dough was not given enough time to double in bulk.
  Too little oil or shortening.

Problem: Dough lacks volume.

Causes: Too much salt.
  Improper mixing (dough hasn't been fully kneaded).
  Not enough yeast; yeast is poor quality; yeast too old.
  Improper proofing.

Problem: Dough tears during rolling or stretching.

Causes: Flour too weak (see "Flour" section).

Dough was given too much rising time.

Dough was undermixed, which means gluten has not been fully developed.

Problem: Dough is too sticky.

Causes: Too much water.

Flour too weak (see "Flour" section).

Dough rose at too high a temperature, causing excess moisture to develop on the surface.

Problem: Dough under the toppings is not cooked or is gummy.

Causes: Oven temperature too low.

Too much cheese or other toppings with too much moisture.

Tomatoes have too much water content.

Cheese has too much fat content.

Flour is too weak (see "Flour" section), making the dough too soft and porous.

Problem: Crust is not brown enough.

Causes: Oven temperature too low.

Not enough sugar in basic recipe.

Dough was too cold going into the oven.

Problem: Crust is too brown.

Causes: Oven temperature too high.

Too much sugar in basic recipe.

Problem:	Crust has poor flavor.
Causes:	Not enough salt.
	Dough too old (young doughs should have a sweeter taste; older doughs have a tendency to be slightly sour).
	Improper dough conditioning (mixing and kneading process was not followed).

Problem:	Baked crust is not crisp enough.
Causes:	Too much sugar.
	Too much shortening or oil.
	Too much water.
	Oven temperature too low.

FLOUR

All-Purpose Flour

Flour is categorized as either strong or weak, depending on the amount of gluten that can be developed in the flour. Gluten is formed when flour is combined with water. High-quality gluten is very elastic and can easily double in bulk without tearing or breaking down; hence stretchability and elasticity of the dough are a function of the gluten. Flour with high-quality gluten is called *strong* flour and is made from hard wheat. It is high in protein, 13 to 14 percent, and it is the flour preferred for yeast doughs. In weak flours the gluten is lower in quality and quantity. Weak flours are low in protein, 11 percent or less, and are best for making pastry, cakes, and cookies.

In Italy, pizzamakers prefer to use OO-grade hard flour, which gives the pizza a good chew but makes the crust tender without a hint of toughness. The closest approximation of OO flour in this country is bread flour, which is high in protein and thus gluten and can be used in any of the dough recipes in this book. However, because of its high protein content, a dough made with bread flour must be kneaded longer (in a stand mixer, for example) and with more vigor (if by hand) than a basic all-purpose flour to develop the gluten. Failure to do this will result in a very dense, not very tender dough, one that will be hard to roll out or stretch. For this reason the dough recipes in this book call for unbleached all-purpose flour. It does the job well, and it will produce an excellent pizza dough.

Whole-Wheat Flour

Pizza dough can be made using only whole-wheat flour, but I wouldn't recommend doing so, because it will produce a flat, dense crust with an unappealing flavor. In this book, therefore, whole-wheat flour is used only in small amounts, to add color and a hint of whole-wheat flavor.

Semolina Flour

Semolina or durum semolina is the hardest wheat grown, a fact that makes it perfect for pasta but too hard by itself for pizza dough. However, a small amount of semolina flour (no more than 1 cup of semolina to every 3 cups of all-purpose flour) works fine. The result? A crust that is a bit richer-tasting with a slightly different texture and chewiness. Also, the finished product will have a hint of yellow.

YEAST

Yeast is a living one-celled plant. It needs food like any other living plant or animal if it is to work properly. In the making of pizza dough, the food is supplied by flour and water. Without yeast you cannot make pizza dough or any other bakery product that requires leavening. Without leavening action, which is the ability of the dough to form gases and rise, pizza dough would be dense, heavy, and very unappetizing.

The leavening action of yeast works like this: The action of the yeast enzymes causes the splitting of the natural sugars found in flour. This causes the formation of carbon dioxide and alcohol. It is the carbon dioxide—a gas—trapped within the gluten structure that causes the dough to rise.

Though most recipes in this book call for active dry yeast, several other forms are available.

Active Dry Yeast

Active dry yeast comes in ¼-ounce envelopes (2½ teaspoons) or in jars. If you bake a lot and can get active dry yeast in a jar, this is a more economical way to buy it. When measuring from the jar, the teaspoon should be completely level or, better yet, 1 level tablespoon will do the job of one packet of yeast. Be sure to check the expiration date on the package or jar before using.

Instant Active Dry Yeast

Also known as *rapid-rise* or *quick-rise yeast*, this yeast comes in ¼-ounce packages, too. Essentially it speeds up the fermentation process—by about 50 percent—and can be used in any of the recipes in this book should you need pizza dough in a hurry. However, I prefer the slower, easy rise of regular active dry yeast or fresh yeast, especially when the dough is allowed to rise overnight in the refrigerator, because it yields a dough with better flavor and better texture.

Fresh or Cake Yeast

This is still the preferred yeast of a lot of bread bakers and some old-world pizzamakers. It has a short shelf life and should always be refrigerated. Though I know some pizzamakers who simply crumble this yeast into the flour, even before adding water, it's better to dissolve it in water before mixing it into the flour to assure even distribution. To substitute fresh yeast for the recipes in this book, use ¾ ounce of fresh or cake yeast (about 2 tablespoons, crumbled) in place of one envelope of active dry yeast.

Water and Yeast

Yeast doesn't do anything until it comes into contact with water, so it is important to pay attention to water temperature. I keep several instant-read thermometers in my kitchens; they are invaluable when it comes to checking water temperature. Here are some pointers for the water/yeast connection.

- The average water temperature used to rehydrate (dissolve in water) yeast is 105 to 115°F, which is considered lukewarm.

- The hotter the water, the faster the dough will rise. Using cold water to rehydrate yeast will slow the fermentation (pizzamakers who want a dough to last for several days under refrigeration actually use ice-cold water, and sometimes ice cubes, when making pizza dough).

- Yeast is killed at a temperature of 138°F, so never use water hotter than that.

- Manufacturers of instant dry active yeast recommend using a water temperature of 130°F to rehydrate yeast (obviously to get matters moving faster). However, this type of yeast can be blended directly into the flour—it doesn't necessarily need to be rehydrated. But to take full advantage of the "instant" factor, use the 130°F water.

To rehydrate yeast or not has always been a popular question. I rehydrate yeast because I believe that it disperses the yeast more evenly throughout the dough. Is rehydrating absolutely essential to making pizza dough? No. And rehydrating doesn't necessarily make fermentation happen faster—that relates to water temperature—but it does give the yeast a jump start, and to my way of thinking it enhances the fermentation process.

Proofing Yeast

The purpose of dissolving yeast in water (rehydrating) is not so much proofing—testing the yeast to see if it is still alive—but getting the fermentation process off to a good start. However, if you have any doubt about whether the yeast is alive, proofing is an essential step (and some people, like me, do it this way just because of tradition).

To proof yeast, simply sprinkle one envelope of yeast over about ½ cup warm water, add about ¼ teaspoon of sugar, and stir to dissolve. Yeast that is good will foam in 5–10 minutes.

Salt inhibits yeast activity, so don't add any salt to the water at this time.

OILS

Olive Oil

Olive oil adds flavor to pizza dough. It does not perform any shortening function. It's perfectly OK to use pure olive oil instead of extra-virgin in a dough. If you're drizzling olive oil over a baked pizza, however, you will be rewarded by the fruity and rich flavor of extra-virgin oil.

Vegetable Oils

Vegetable oil acts as shortening in pizza dough—more or less depending on the amount used—imparting tenderness and softness to the finished pizza. The dough for Chicago Deep-Dish Pizza, for example, calls for a lot more vegetable oil than would ordinarily be used. This creates a short dough, one that will have a more tender, somewhat flakier crust. Some pizzamakers use a solid shortening such as margarine (and in extreme cases lard) to achieve this effect.

DOUGH ADDITIVES

Some commercial pizza dough makers use dough additives to boost the protein level of a weaker flour, which in turn enhances the flexibility and elasticity of the risen dough. In effect this makes it easier to stretch, throw, slap, and roll the dough without tearing it or poking holes in it.

Now a product very similar to that used in the pizza industry is available for home use. It is called Dough Easy and is a natural by-product of milk processing. The ingredients are whey and L-cysteine (an amino acid that is a natural component of protein). Adding a small amount of this product to a basic pizza dough will improve the handling, making the dough easier to stretch and roll. This product also enhances the crust color of the baked pizza.

Dough Easy is available in selected specialty gourmet stores around the country. If you can't find it, contact the distributor, Kitchen Supply Company, 7333 W. Harrison, Forest Park, IL 60130 (708-383-5990), for pricing and information.

Chapter 2

MAKING PIZZA DOUGH

If you measure your ingredients accurately, each of the following dough recipes will turn out just fine. The dough will be exactly the right consistency—smooth, elastic, easy to knead. Keep in mind, however, that humidity affects the amount of water the flour will absorb—high humidity generally means that you will need slightly less water—so there is always some slight adjustment to be made. Generally it is easier to adjust the consistency of pizza dough by adding flour than by adding water, so always use the exact amount of water called for in the recipe. Then, by gradually adding flour, bring the dough to a smooth, flexible, easy-to-knead mass.

I use one simple test to bring pizza dough to the proper consistency: when I press into the ball of dough with the heel of my hand, I want my hand to come away clean. I am after a dough that is soft and pliable but not the least bit sticky.

When a recipe calls for mixing the dough in a large bowl, you can use a stand mixer. No changes in the method are necessary; the only difference is that the machine will do the kneading. Run the mixer for 5 to 6 minutes at medium-high speed.

ABOUT PROOFING PIZZA DOUGH

In the pizza industry the term *proofing* is applied not only to testing the yeast to make sure it's alive but also to letting the dough rise. When commercial pizzamakers talk about proofing the dough, they mean "allow the dough to double in bulk," as most cookbooks say. The best pizzerias mix the dough the day before they plan to use it. After mixing, they scale the dough (by weight according to the sizes used in that pizzeria), form it into balls, and set them into large proofing trays. Then they stack the trays in a cooler at a temperature of about 38°F.

Though the dough is in a cold environment, fermentation is still taking place—just very slowly. This is known as *retarding the dough.* Dough retardation is a process of slow fermentation and rising over at least 12 hours (with proper mixing and handling the retardation process can be extended for 3 to 4 days) under cold conditions.

The two factors that affect the way dough is proofed are temperature and humidity. In commercial pizza operations it is common to use a proofer, a temperature-controlled cabinet that encloses the dough balls and subjects them to humidity. It is a most effective way to get the perfect dough ball.

OVERNIGHT PIZZA DOUGH

The retardation method, which can be used in any of the dough recipes in this book, produces an excellent dough, because the dough matures gently as it rises slowly in the refrigerator overnight. Several points to keep in mind:

- If you put the dough or dough balls into a bowl or on a cookie sheet, you must cover them in some way—plastic wrap and a kitchen towel, for example. Another method is to put the dough into a floured and tightly sealed plastic freezer bag. The idea is to keep the refrigerator from sucking the moisture from the dough.

- The next day, take the dough out of the refrigerator in plenty of time to bring it to room temperature, generally about 2 hours. Leave it covered in the bowl. Alternatively you can roll or stretch the dough, straight from the refrigerator, into the proper size and place it on the pizza pan, cover it, and bring it to room temperature. Often this is a quicker way of bringing the dough to room temperature.

One of the main reasons that dough tastes heavy after baking, has no texture, or is hard to stretch or roll is that it is not given enough time to rise fully. This is true whether the dough is made and used the same day or is retarded in the refrigerator overnight.

THE CRUST QUESTION: HOW THIN IS THIN?

The thinness or thickness of pizza crust is determined by the rolling or pressing of the dough. For example, dough made with 3 cups of flour and 1 cup of liquid will yield about 1½ pounds of dough, which will make two pizza shells or crusts 12 to 13 inches in diameter. The rule of thumb for a pizza of average thickness is 1 ounce of dough for each inch of crust diameter desired.

Suppose, however, you want a pizza with a thinner crust. Simply divide the same 1½ pounds of dough into three equal pieces and roll each to a diameter of, say, 9 to 10 inches. Getting a super thin or cracker crust is simply a matter of rolling the dough even thinner. I've been in pizza restaurants where ¼ pound of dough is used to make an 8-inch pizza.

PIZZA POINTER

You can alter the appearance of your pizza by simply using your hands or fingers. For example, by pressing the edge of the dough with your fingers—in effect pinching it to form a ridge—the baked pizza will have a "frame" around the crust. A smaller pinch, a smaller frame; a larger pinch, a larger frame.

Also, how far you extend the toppings toward the edge of the crust will affect the amount of crust that you will see and eat. Keep in mind that any part of the pizza dough not covered by toppings will rise a lot higher than the area covered by toppings.

FREEZING DOUGH

Pizza dough takes very well to freezing. Make the dough and allow it to rise for at least an hour. Punch it down, form it into a ball, place it in a plastic freezer bag, and freeze. It will be good in the freezer for up to three months. To use, remove the bag from the freezer the night before you plan to use it and put it in the refrigerator. Take the dough out of the refrigerator (leave it in the bag) about 1 hour before you plan to bake it. When you're ready to go, remove the dough from the plastic bag, lightly flour the work surface, roll the dough to the desired size, place it on a pizza pan, cover it with plastic wrap, and let it come to room temperature.

BAKING PIZZA

There are several viable options for baking pizza: flat pizza pans made of heavyweight aluminum or steel, pizza screens, heavyweight cookie sheets or jelly-roll pans, and a baking stone. Any of these will work just fine and do the job, but each has its own baking characteristics. For example, the baking stone does a great job of giving a pizza a crispy crust. Suffice it to say that I invented the very first baking stone in 1973, so I know what it can do. The only problem with the stone is that you need a pizza peel or paddle to get the pizza on and off the stone, and this takes a little practice, but it's well worth the effort.

The flat pizza pans are the easiest to use. I always rub a thin layer of cooking oil over the surface, especially when the pan is new, to make sure the dough doesn't stick. Once the pan is well used and seasoned, the oil isn't necessary.

The pizza screen is a good idea because it does help to develop a crispier crust. Be careful, though, because the crust might start to crisp up well before the cheese is melted and bubbly, which means you should move the pizza from the bottom rack to the middle of the oven.

I often use a cookie sheet or jelly-roll pan when I'm baking two small pizzas. I put the pizza shells on the pan, add the toppings, and bake. Easy on, easy off.

TIPS FOR USING
THE BAKING STONE

When I wrote my first pizza cookbook (*The Great Chicago-Style Pizza Cookbook*) over 10 years ago, I advocated using cornmeal on the pizza peel for sliding the pizza onto the baking stone. That method still works, provided you use enough cornmeal and don't end up with most of it on the baking stone or on the oven floor. Flouring the pizza peel is a viable option and creates less of a mess.

A brand-new pizza peel, though it may look and feel smooth, still has enough of a rough surface to grab the dough and prevent the crust from sliding off. Season your pizza peel by rubbing flour into the surface with your hand, making circles as you rub. This helps to smooth out some of those invisible rough spots on the peel.

To practice using a pizza peel, fold a kitchen towel into a square and place it on the unfloured peel. With a series of small and even jerks, try to slide the towel onto a large plate set on your kitchen counter. A pizza with but a few toppings is usually not a problem, but when a pizza is loaded the challenge of getting it off the peel and onto the baking stone is ever present.

As insurance, place the pizza shell on the floured peel and jerk the peel back and forth to be sure that the shell moves freely. Put on the toppings and once again, before heading for the oven, make sure the pizza is moving freely on the peel.

The hotter the stone, the better your crust will turn out, so preheat the stone for 30 minutes. Put the baking stone in the oven before you turn it on to preheat. After you've made sure your pizza is moving freely on the peel, lay the edge of the peel on the stone toward the very back. Using short, swift jerks, slide the pizza onto the hot stone.

PARBAKING A PIZZA CRUST

If you're having a pizza party and wish to get a jump on the preparations, it's feasible and practical to parbake the crust. Roll or stretch the dough as directed in the recipe. Pierce the base of the pizza shell all over—except for the border—with the tines of a fork (in a pizza restaurant a dough docker, a rolling device with spikes on a wheel, is used for this purpose). Bake the pizza shell in a preheated 500°F oven for 4 minutes to set the crust. Allow the crust to cool for 10 minutes before topping. The crust can be parbaked and held for several hours, or held overnight in the refrigerator, or wrapped and frozen for later use. To use the crust from the freezer, allow it to thaw completely at room temperature before making a pizza.

Parbaking the crust is also advisable when a pizza recipe calls for a number of toppings or for heavy toppings. Parbaking prevents the crust from getting soggy as it might if the toppings release an unusual amount of moisture. Several recipes in this book recommend this step.

PIZZA ON THE GRILL

Grilled pizza has become a sensation over the last few years, and when done right it is absolutely delicious. I started grilling pizza some years ago in the backyard of our Wisconsin summer house, doing weekend lunches for my wife and me. It wasn't long, though, before I was placing the technique into commercial application for some of my clients.

My backyard approach is pretty straightforward. I get the charcoal to the point where the coals are gray and hot. Next I press out a ball of risen pizza dough until it is about ⅛ inch thick. An easy method for doing this is to put about 2 teaspoons of olive oil on the kitchen counter or a flat pizza pan and rub it lightly into a circle about the same diameter as the pizza you plan to make. Now flatten the ball of dough on the oil and press and turn your hands, pushing and stretching until the dough gets to the right size.

Next I brush olive oil lightly over both sides of the dough. Now I flop the pizza shell directly onto the grill—carefully so the dough doesn't fall through onto the coals. In about 30 seconds the dough starts to puff. Using tongs, I move the dough around, turning it once or twice until the dough is grilled and light brown on one side, about 2 minutes. I flip it over and brown the other side, another 2 minutes.

Off the grill, I top the pizza with a mixture of diced fresh tomatoes, cuttings of fresh basil, olive oil, salt, and pepper. Sometimes I sprinkle on grated Parmesan cheese; sometimes I toss small cubes of fontina or provolone cheese with the tomatoes. The flavor is great.

Try it, using the recipe for Basic Pizza Dough II.

Pizza Trivia

Americans spend $25 billion a year on pizza, which amounts to an average of 25 pounds per person per year or something like 100 million slices per month.

Chapter 3

PIZZA DOUGH RECIPES

PAT'S FAVORITE PIZZA DOUGH

This is a straightforward pizza dough, one that I have been using for years, and it's foolproof. Always make the full recipe. If you wish to make only one pizza, freeze one of the dough balls after the dough has had one rise.

Makes two 13- to 14-inch pizza shells

> 1 ¼-ounce envelope (2½ teaspoons) active dry yeast
> 1 teaspoon sugar
> 1 cup warm water (105–115°F)
> 2 tablespoons olive oil
> 1 teaspoon salt
> 3¼ to 3½ cups unbleached all-purpose flour

In a large bowl, combine the yeast with the sugar and water. Let stand for 10 minutes or until it is foamy. Stir in the olive oil and salt.

Add 3¼ cups of the flour and blend the mixture, incorporating as much of the remaining ¼ cup flour as necessary to prevent the dough from sticking. At this point the dough should be soft and pliable and clean the sides of the bowl.

Turn the dough out of the bowl onto a work surface and knead for 6–8 minutes or until it is smooth and elastic.

Put the dough in an oiled bowl and turn it twice to coat. Cover the bowl with plastic wrap and a kitchen towel. Set the bowl in a warm place and allow to rise for 1½ hours or until it has doubled in bulk.

Punch it down and divide the dough in half. Roll or stretch each piece into a 13- to 14-inch circle about ⅛ inch thick. Transfer the dough to a lightly oiled 14- to 15-inch-diameter flat pizza pan or pizza screen or to a lightly floured pizza peel if you're using a baking stone.

BASIC FOOD PROCESSOR PIZZA DOUGH

Essentially the same dough as Pat's Favorite, except cool water is used because the food processor generates a lot of heat of its own. So if hot water were used, the temperature might rise to the point of killing the yeast.

Makes two 13- to 14-inch pizza shells

    1 ¼-ounce envelope (2½ teaspoons) active dry yeast
    1 teaspoon sugar
    1 cup cool water
    2 tablespoons olive oil
    3¼ to 3½ cups unbleached all-purpose flour
    1 teaspoon salt

In a glass measuring cup or small bowl, combine the yeast with the sugar and water. Let stand for 10 minutes or until it is foamy. Stir in the olive oil.

Put 3¼ cups of the flour and the salt in the food processor and process for 5 seconds. Add the yeast mixture and process the mixture until it forms a ball, adding the additional ¼ cup of flour 1 tablespoon at a time until the dough forms a ball and is no longer sticky. Process the dough for 15–20 seconds.

Turn the dough out of the processor onto a work surface and knead for 1 minute or until it is smooth and elastic.

Put the dough in an oiled bowl and turn it twice to coat it with the oil. Cover the bowl with plastic wrap and a kitchen towel. Set the bowl in a warm place and allow to rise for 1 hour or until it has doubled in bulk.

Punch it down and divide the dough in half. Roll or stretch each piece into a 13- to 14-inch circle about ⅛ inch thick. Transfer the dough to a lightly oiled 14- to 15-inch-diameter flat pizza pan or pizza screen or to a lightly floured pizza peel if you're using a baking stone.

BASIC PIZZA DOUGH II

Use this recipe if you wish to make a scaled-down version of Pat's Favorite. Don't try to cut a dough recipe in half; things can get a little out of hand with the flour and water.

Makes one 14-inch pizza shell

> 1 ¼-ounce envelope (2½ teaspoons) active dry yeast
> ⅔ cup warm water (105–115°F)
> ½ teaspoon sugar
> 2 tablespoons olive oil
> ½ teaspoon salt
> 2 to 2¼ cups unbleached all-purpose flour

In a large bowl, combine the yeast with the water and sugar and let stand for 10 minutes or until it is foamy. Add the olive oil and salt and stir to combine.

Add 2 cups of the flour and blend the mixture, incorporating as much of the additional ¼ cup of flour as necessary to form a nonsticky dough.

Turn the dough out of the bowl onto a work surface and knead for 6–8 minutes or until it is smooth and elastic.

Put the dough in an oiled bowl and turn it twice to coat it with the oil. Cover the bowl with plastic wrap and a kitchen towel. Set the bowl in a warm place and allow to rise for 1 hour or until it has doubled in bulk. Do not punch it down.

Lift the ball of dough gently from the bowl. On a lightly floured surface, roll the dough into a 14-inch circle about ⅛ inch thick. Transfer the dough to a lightly oiled 14- to 15-inch-diameter flat pizza pan or pizza screen or to a lightly floured pizza peel if you're using a baking stone.

QUICK-RISING DOUGH

If you want pizza dough in about 45 minutes, use this recipe. The dough will be softer and will not have the same texture as a dough made with regular yeast or a dough that rises in the refrigerator overnight. Nevertheless it does the job.

Makes one 14-inch pizza shell

> 1 ¼-ounce envelope quick-rise yeast
> 2 to 2¼ cups unbleached all-purpose flour
> 1 teaspoon sugar
> ½ teaspoon salt
> ⅔ cup hot water (125–130°F)
> 2 tablespoons olive oil

In a large bowl, blend the yeast with 2 cups of the flour, the sugar, and the salt. Slowly add the water, followed by the olive oil. Combine the mixture until a ragged mass of dough is formed, incorporating as much of the additional ¼ cup of flour as necessary to make a nonsticky ball of dough.

Turn the dough out of the bowl onto a work surface and knead vigorously for 6–8 minutes or until it is smooth and elastic.

Put the dough in an oiled bowl and turn it twice to coat it with the oil. Cover the bowl with plastic wrap and a kitchen towel. Set the bowl in a warm place and allow to rise for 25–30 minutes. Do not punch it down.

Lift the ball of dough gently from the bowl and, on a lightly floured surface, stretch or roll the dough into a 13- to 14-inch circle about ⅛ inch thick. Transfer the dough to a lightly oiled 14- to 15-inch-diameter flat pizza pan or pizza screen or to a lightly floured pizza peel if you're using a baking stone.

PIZZA POINTER

It is easy to make two pizzas where a dough recipe calls for only one. In cases where a recipe uses a particular dough recipe—Basic Pizza Dough II, which makes one 14-inch pizza, for example—substitute Pat's Favorite Pizza Dough, which makes two large pizzas. After that it's just a matter of doubling the toppings.

BEER CRUST

Using beer to make a pizza dough is nothing new; beer froth was used as a leavening agent in ancient Egypt, and a lot of pizzerias today use beer as their "secret ingredient." Using beer as one of the liquids accomplishes two things: it enhances the fermentation, resulting in a dough that has excellent texture, and the malt in the beer, working with the other ingredients, helps produce a golden brown crust.

This dough has more body when made the night before and allowed to rise slowly in the refrigerator overnight. The next day, take it out of the refrigerator at least 2 hours before you plan to use it. There is no odor or taste of beer after the crust is baked.

Makes two 12-inch pizza shells

> ½ cup warm water (105–115°F)
> 1 ¼-ounce envelope (2½ teaspoons) active dry yeast
> ¼ cup warm beer
> 1 teaspoon sugar
> 2¾ to 3 cups unbleached all-purpose flour
> 2 teaspoons salt

In a large bowl, combine the water, yeast, beer, and sugar. Stir well to combine. Let stand for 10 minutes or until it is foamy.

Add 2¾ cups of the flour and the salt to the yeast mixture and blend, incorporating as much of the remaining ¼ cup of flour as necessary to prevent the dough from sticking.

Turn the dough out of the bowl onto a lightly floured work surface and knead for 6–8 minutes or until it is smooth and elastic.

Put the dough in an oiled bowl and turn it twice to coat it with the oil. Cover the bowl with plastic wrap and a kitchen towel and place it in the refrigerator to rise overnight. (Alternatively, let the dough rise in a warm place for 1½ hours or until it has doubled in bulk and punch it down.)

The next day, remove the dough from the refrigerator at least 2 hours before you plan to use it. Then divide the dough in half and roll or stretch each piece into a 12-inch circle about ⅛ inch (or slightly less) thick. Transfer the dough to a lightly oiled 12- to 13-inch-diameter flat pizza pan or pizza screen or to a lightly floured pizza peel if you're using a baking stone.

FRIDAY NIGHT PIZZA DOUGH

This is the dough recipe I use when I'm planning a pizza party on a Saturday afternoon or evening. The name comes from the fact that my mother always made homemade pizza on Saturday, sometimes starting the dough the night before. The initial sponge mixture gives this pizza dough a jump start, resulting in a lighter texture.

Makes two 14- to 15-inch pizza shells

FIRST RISING (SPONGE)

½ ounce fresh yeast
½ cup warm water
heaped ½ cup bread flour

In a large bowl, dissolve the yeast in the water. Stir in the flour. Let the sponge stand, uncovered, for 1 hour.

SECOND RISING

3½ cups unbleached all-purpose flour
2 teaspoons salt
1 cup warm water (105–115°F)

Add to the sponge mixture the flour, salt, and water. Blend and knead the mixture in the bowl until a dough is formed. The dough will feel slightly moist. Turn the dough out of the bowl onto a lightly floured surface and knead vigorously for 6–8 minutes or until it is smooth and elastic.

Divide the dough into two equal pieces of 1 pound each and roll and form each piece into a compact ball. Lightly dust the inside of two large plastic freezer bags with flour and place one ball of dough in each bag. Put the bags in the refrigerator overnight.

The next day, at least 1 hour before you plan to bake the pizzas, remove the bags from the refrigerator and the dough from the bags (the dough can be punched down and frozen at this point).

On a lightly floured surface, roll or stretch each piece of dough into a 14- to 15-inch circle about ⅛ inch thick. Transfer the dough to a lightly oiled 14- to 15-inch-diameter flat pizza pan or pizza screen. Cover the dough with plastic wrap and a kitchen towel and let sit in a warm place for 1 hour before topping and baking.

UNLEAVENED PIZZA DOUGH

If time is a problem, here is a dough that is ready to go in no time flat. Because it is unleavened, there is no texture to speak of, so it is best to roll the dough extra-thin.

Makes two 13- to 14-inch pizza shells or four 7-inch pizza shells

>   *2 cups unbleached all-purpose flour*
>   *1 teaspoon salt*
>   *2 tablespoons olive oil*
>   *⅔ cup warm water*

In a mixing bowl, combine the flour and salt. Stir in the olive oil and water. Blend the mixture until it forms a dough. Knead the dough on a lightly floured surface for 2–3 minutes or until it is smooth and elastic (the dough can be refrigerated at this point for up to 3 days).

Divide the dough in half (or into four pieces for 7-inch pizzas). On a lightly floured surface, roll each piece into a 13- to 14-inch circle that is almost paper-thin. Transfer the dough to a lightly oiled 14- to 15-inch-diameter flat pizza pan or pizza screen or to a lightly floured pizza peel if you're using a baking stone.

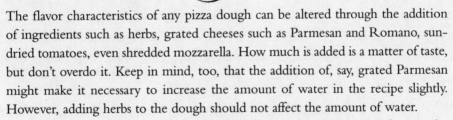

PIZZA POINTER

The flavor characteristics of any pizza dough can be altered through the addition of ingredients such as herbs, grated cheeses such as Parmesan and Romano, sun-dried tomatoes, even shredded mozzarella. How much is added is a matter of taste, but don't overdo it. Keep in mind, too, that the addition of, say, grated Parmesan might make it necessary to increase the amount of water in the recipe slightly. However, adding herbs to the dough should not affect the amount of water.

Regardless of the flavor enhancer you use, always add it to the flour in the mixing bowl and be sure to combine it thoroughly and evenly.

WHOLE-WHEAT PIZZA DOUGH

Use this dough recipe if you're having a pizza party and wish to make several pizzas with various toppings. This recipe also works very nicely as an overnight dough.

Makes two 12-inch pizza shells or four 8- to 9-inch shells

> ½ cup warm water (105–115°F)
> 1 ¼-ounce envelope (2½ teaspoons) active dry yeast
> 2 teaspoons honey
> 2 tablespoons olive oil
> 2½ cups unbleached all-purpose flour
> ½ cup whole-wheat flour
> 1 teaspoon salt
> ¾ cup cool water

In a large bowl, combine the water, yeast, and honey. Stir to dissolve the yeast. Let stand for 10 minutes or until it is foamy. Stir in the olive oil.

Add the flours and salt to the bowl and stir to combine. Add the cool water. Blend and mix until a dough is formed.

Turn the dough out of the bowl onto a work surface and knead for 6–8 minutes or until it is smooth and elastic.

Place the dough in a lightly oiled bowl, turning it twice to coat it with the oil. Cover the bowl with plastic wrap and a kitchen towel. Let rise for 45 minutes.

Punch down the dough. Divide and shape it into two or four equal balls. Place the dough balls into lightly floured plastic freezer bags (or on a cookie sheet and cover tightly with plastic wrap) and refrigerate for 2 hours or overnight. Remove the dough from the refrigerator at least 1 hour before baking.

SWEET PIZZA DOUGH

A simple and easy dough to make and use for sweet pizza. The dough can be made by hand, with a stand mixer, or in a food processor. Press the dough into a circle that is about 13 inches in diameter; however, when you form the crust border (or a braid as suggested in the Pizza Pointer), the size will be reduced by 1 inch.

Makes one 12-inch pizza

> ½ cup warm water (105–115°F)
> 1 ¼-ounce envelope (2½ teaspoons) active dry yeast
> 2 teaspoons honey
> 1¾ cups all-purpose flour
> ¼ teaspoon salt

Measure the water in a glass measuring cup. Sprinkle the yeast over the water and add the honey. Stir well to combine and dissolve. Let stand for 10 minutes or until it foams.

Place the flour and salt in a mixing bowl or the bowl of a food processor fitted with the steel blade. Combine. Add the yeast mixture to the flour and combine to form a dough. Knead the dough for 6–7 minutes, until it is soft, smooth, and pliable but not sticky. (If you're using the food processor, process for 1 minute after the dough forms a ball; remove from the machine and knead by hand for 1 minute.)

Place the dough in a lightly floured bowl and cover with plastic wrap and a kitchen towel. Allow the dough to rise in a warm place for 1½ hours.

Lift the dough gently from the bowl—*do not punch it down*—by sliding your hand under it. Place the dough on a lightly floured work surface and with your hands press and push it into a circle about 13 inches in diameter. Transfer the dough to a flat pizza pan or lightly floured pizza peel.

PIZZA POINTER

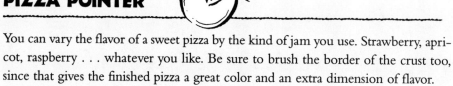

You can vary the flavor of a sweet pizza by the kind of jam you use. Strawberry, apricot, raspberry . . . whatever you like. Be sure to brush the border of the crust too, since that gives the finished pizza a great color and an extra dimension of flavor.

To give the border of the crust a more appealing look, indent and curl the crust border with your thumb and forefinger to form a braid—before you brush on the jam.

Or . . .

To add an extra element of flavor to a pizza dough, infuse it with herbs. In the Basic Pizza Dough II recipe, add the following ingredients to the flour in step 2: 1 tablespoon minced fresh rosemary (or 1 teaspoon dried), 1 tablespoon minced fresh basil (or 1 teaspoon dried), and 1 tablespoon minced fresh oregano (or 1 teaspoon dried).

Chapter 4

SAUCES

WORKING WITH TOMATOES

Even in the best of times (and months) getting fresh plum tomatoes that are truly ripe can be a problem. The viable alternative is of course canned plum tomatoes. A number of brands—imported and domestic—are on the market, and at one time or another I've tried them all. If price is no object, the choice is clear: any canned plum tomato that has the name San Marzano on the label is the way to go. These are tomatoes grown and packed in and around Naples and are the most perfect example of how a true Italian tomato should taste. You can find them in gourmet food markets and Italian food markets.

As far as domestic brands are concerned, try one kind or another, and when you find one you like, stay with it. Stay away from brands that tend to pack unripe, misshapen tomatoes. Domestic brands are usually labeled "Italian-style plum tomatoes," so that's what my recipes call for, but of course San Marzano tomatoes won't say that—they are *real* Italian.

In the recipes where I use the tomatoes straight from the can as opposed to making a cooked sauce, there's a danger of too much water coming from the tomatoes, making a soggy pizza crust. So I suggest in each instance that the tomatoes be opened, drained, crushed by hand—either in the can or in a mixing bowl—and drained again. Of course this will reduce the amount of coverage that the tomatoes will give, but it's worth it.

I do not recommend putting the tomatoes in the food processor; this will puree them, not crush them, and a puree is not what we're after in the recipes that use canned plum tomatoes.

TOMATO SAUCES FOR PIZZAS

In addition to the tomatoes—fresh and canned—used in the various pizza recipes, here are several cooked tomato sauces that will add another taste dimension to pizza. Any one of these sauces can be substituted in the recipes calling for tomatoes.

Should you need a larger quantity, any of these sauce recipes can be doubled.

Special Note: Some stores carry 35-ounce cans of plum tomatoes. Use the 35-ounce can in the sauce recipes that follow. The extra 7 ounces will give even better tomato coverage for two pizzas.

FRAGRANT TOMATO SAUCE

Makes about 2 cups or enough sauce for two 13- to 14-inch pizzas

1 large clove garlic, minced
1 tablespoon extra-virgin olive oil
1 28-ounce can Italian-style plum tomatoes
⅛ teaspoon freshly ground black pepper
Pinch of sugar
Salt to taste

In a large heavy saucepan, sauté the garlic in the olive oil over moderate heat for 2 minutes.

Empty the tomatoes and their juices into a mixing bowl and crush the tomatoes with your hands. Add the tomatoes to the saucepan. Add the pepper and sugar. Bring the sauce to a boil over medium-high heat. Cook the sauce at a steady simmer, stirring occasionally, for 18–20 minutes or until it has thickened and reduced to about 2 cups. Add salt to taste. The sauce can be prepared ahead and will keep, covered and refrigerated, for 4–5 days. The sauce can also be frozen. Let the sauce cool for at least 30 minutes before using it on pizza.

Pizza Trivia

The Italian name for the raised edge or border referred to in the recipes in this book is *il cornicione* or "large frame."

HERBED TOMATO SAUCE

Makes about 2 cups or enough sauce for two 13- to 14-inch pizzas

1 large clove garlic, minced
1 tablespoon extra-virgin olive oil
1 28-ounce can Italian-style plum tomatoes
⅛ teaspoon freshly ground black pepper
¼ teaspoon dried oregano, crumbled
¼ teaspoon dried basil, crumbled, or 1 tablespoon fresh, torn
1 tablespoon chopped fresh parsley
Salt to taste

In a large heavy saucepan, sauté the garlic in the oil over moderate heat for 2 minutes.

Empty the tomatoes and their juices into a mixing bowl and crush the tomatoes with your hands. Add the tomatoes to the saucepan. Add the pepper, oregano, basil, and parsley. Bring the sauce to a boil over medium-high heat. Cook the sauce at a steady simmer, stirring occasionally, for 18–20 minutes or until the sauce has thickened and reduced to about 2 cups. Add salt to taste. The sauce can be prepared ahead and will keep, covered and refrigerated, for 4–5 days. The sauce can also be frozen. Let the sauce cool for at least 30 minutes before using it on pizza.

SPICY TOMATO SAUCE

Makes about 2 cups or enough sauce for two 13- to 14-inch pizzas

> *1 large clove garlic, minced*
> *1 tablespoon extra-virgin olive oil*
> *1 28-ounce can Italian-style plum tomatoes*
> *¼ teaspoon freshly ground black pepper*
> *1 tablespoon chopped fresh oregano or ½ teaspoon dried, crumbled*
> *¼ teaspoon Tabasco sauce*
> *Salt to taste*

In a large heavy saucepan, sauté the garlic in the oil over moderate heat for 2 minutes.

Empty the tomatoes and their juices into a mixing bowl and crush the tomatoes with your hands. Add the tomatoes to the saucepan. Add the pepper, oregano, and Tabasco sauce. Bring the sauce to a boil over medium-high heat. Cook the sauce at a steady simmer, stirring occasionally, for 18–20 minutes or until the sauce has thickened and reduced to about 2 cups. Add salt to taste. The sauce can be prepared ahead and will keep, covered and refrigerated, for 4–5 days. The sauce can also be frozen. Let the sauce cool for at least 30 minutes before using it on pizza.

EXTRA-SPICY TOMATO SAUCE

Makes 2 cups or enough sauce for two 13- to 14-inch pizzas

> *1 large clove garlic, minced*
> *1 tablespoon extra-virgin olive oil*
> *1 28-ounce can Italian-style plum tomatoes*
> *⅛ teaspoon freshly ground black pepper*
> *½ tablespoon chopped fresh oregano or ¼ teaspoon dried, crumbled*
> *1 tablespoon chopped chipotle peppers in adobo sauce**
> *Salt to taste*

In a large heavy saucepan, sauté the garlic in the oil over moderate heat for 2 minutes.

Empty the tomatoes and their juices into a mixing bowl and crush the tomatoes with your hands. Add the tomatoes to the saucepan. Add the pepper, oregano, and chipotles to the tomatoes. Bring the sauce to a boil over medium-high heat. Cook the sauce at a steady simmer, stirring occasionally, for 18–20 minutes or until the sauce has thickened and reduced to about 2 cups. Add salt to taste. The sauce can be prepared ahead and will keep, covered and refrigerated, for 4–5 days. The sauce can also be frozen. Let the sauce cool for at least 30 minutes before using it on pizza.

---

* Use caution when working with the chipotle peppers. Remove them from the can with a fork, place them on a plate, and chop them with a knife and fork. If you have to touch the peppers with your hands, use rubber gloves. The smoky flavor of the chipotle is what makes this sauce. However, if canned chipotle peppers are not available, use fresh jalapeños.

Pizza Trivia

Try using a bottled salsa to zip some additional flavor into a pizza sauce. I prefer using a thick and chunky mild salsa, but with the great variety of salsas on the market the possible taste variations are extensive.

Chapter 5

OTHER INGREDIENTS

CHEESE

There is no end to the possibilities that the pizza-cheese connection offers. In the United States the range of cheeses from Wisconsin, for example, that work with pizza is deep, delicious, and most appealing. Likewise, the great variety of cheeses from Italy can be used with the assurance that the flavor of just about any pizza will be enhanced superbly. Here is the short list of cheeses that go well with pizza. Principal producing countries are noted in parentheses. Don't hesitate to experiment, blending or substituting cheeses that you are particularly fond of.

Asiago (United States and Italy): Cow's milk cheese. Pleasant and mild fragrance. Quite savory.

Caciocavallo (Italy): Hard cow's milk cheese in ball or pear shape. Sweet when young; piquant and spicy when mature.

Feta (United States and Greece): Original Greek feta is made from ewe's milk, while U.S. and other versions are made from cow's milk. Sharp, salty, crumbly.

Fontina (Italy), *fontina* and *fontinella* (United States): Cow's milk cheese. Mild flavor, light yet tangy. Melts well.

Gorgonzola (United States and Italy): Cow's milk cheese. Soft and creamy. Green-blue mold veins. Savory, strong aroma. Use sparingly.

Gouda (United States and the Netherlands): Cow's milk cheese. Mild and buttery. Smooth and firm texture.

Manchego (Spain): Cow's milk cheese. Delightfully tasty, firm yet creamy. Can be grated or eaten as a dessert cheese.

Mascarpone (United States and Italy): Cow's milk cheese. Rich, sweet, smooth, creamy (it's virtually solidified cream). Originally produced only in Lombardy, but now produced in Wisconsin and Vermont as well.

Mozzarella (United States): Cow's milk cheese available part-skim or whole milk. Creamy white, firm texture, delicate milky flavor. Usually sold in plastic-encased 1-pound balls.

Mozzarella di bufala (Italy): Made from the milk of the water buffalo. Hard to find in the United States. Pure white, delicately flavored with a bit of tang. Sold in balls (packed in brine when available in the United States). Best when used as fresh as possible.

Fresh mozzarella aka *fior di latte* (United States): A hand-crafted cow's milk cheese. Firm, creamy-white. Delicate flavor and rich texture. Sold in various sizes and shapes: ciliegine (cherries), small balls of about ½ ounce or less; bocconcino (bite-size) in various sizes. Larger balls, sometimes locally made, can be found in specialty food markets. Keep unused cheese refrigerated and covered with a saltwater solution to prevent spoiling.

Smoked mozzarella (United States and Italy): Cow's milk cheese. A lightly smoked (affumicata) version of mozzarella.

Parmesan (United States): Cow's milk cheese. Semihard, pale yellow in color. Delicate and mild flavor. It is not aged and cured in the same fashion as Parmigiano-Reggiano.

Parmigiano-Reggiano (Italy): Cow's milk cheese made in specially designated cheese-producing zones in Italy. Semihard, yellow, aged. Delicate and fragrant with a most appealing, slightly fruity flavor.

Pecorino Romano (Italy): A ripened sheep's milk cheese. Semihard, used mostly for grating. Sharp, aromatic.

Provolone (United States and Italy): Cow's milk cheese. Firm and grainy (it does become harder with age). Depending on how it is aged, the flavor runs from sweet to savory to hearty and spicy. Sometimes available smoked.

Ricotta (United States and Italy): Cow's milk cheese. Traditionally made from whey but now available made from skim milk. Soft, smooth, with a suggestion of sweetness. Sometimes available in dried form and sold as ricotta salata.

Romano (United States): Cow's milk cheese. Hard, used for grating. Aromatic flavor, but not as sharp as true Pecorino Romano.

Scamorza (United States and Italy): Cow's milk cheese. In Italy it is made in the Abruzzi. Very similar in flavor to mozzarella, but a bit more piquant. Characteristic dimple on one end.

Taleggio (Italy): Cow's milk cheese. Soft and moist. Mild with a hint of tartness. Shaped into traditional and distinctive flat squares.

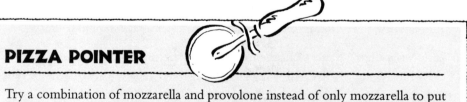

PIZZA POINTER

Try a combination of mozzarella and provolone instead of only mozzarella to put a different flavor spin on a pizza.

OIL

BASIL OLIVE OIL

Brush this oil over unbaked pizza dough before putting on the toppings to give a pizza an essence of basil, drizzle some of the oil over the tomato topping just before baking, or add to the Pizza alla Pesto on page 64 for flavor.

Makes 1 quart

> *3 cups loosely packed fresh basil leaves (no stems)*
> *1 quart olive oil*

Rinse the basil well, shake off excess water, and pat dry between paper towels. Pack the basil loosely into a 1-quart glass jar with a lid. Slowly pour in the oil and let the mixture stand, covered, in a cool dark place for 2 weeks.

Strain the oil, discarding the basil leaves, return the oil to the original jar, and seal the jar with the lid. Store the oil in a cool dark place for up to about 2 months.

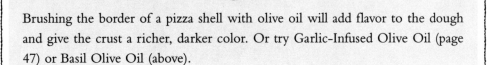

PIZZA POINTER

Brushing the border of a pizza shell with olive oil will add flavor to the dough and give the crust a richer, darker color. Or try Garlic-Infused Olive Oil (page 47) or Basil Olive Oil (above).

PASQUALE'S PIZZA OIL

An all-purpose flavored oil that adds another dimension of flavor when sprinkled on pizza. I use the oil on salads, bruschetta, and grilled bread rubbed with garlic too. You can vary the heat of the oil by changing the type and amount of chili used and the length of time the chilies are left in the oil.

For pizza, sprinkle some of the oil, to taste, over a pizza fresh from the oven. The oil works particularly well with tomato-based and vegetable pizzas.

Makes 3 cups

> *3 cups extra-virgin olive oil*
> *5 tablespoons black peppercorns*
> *2 sprigs fresh rosemary*
> *3 sprigs fresh thyme*
> *3 sprigs fresh oregano*
> *3 whole 2- to 3-inch chilies, crushed (wear rubber gloves)*

Combine the ingredients in a glass jar or bottle with a tight-fitting lid. Let stand in a cool dark place for 2 weeks.

Remove the rosemary, oregano, and thyme and discard. You may also strain the oil at this point and discard the peppercorns and chilies. The oil will keep in a cool dark place for about 6 weeks.

GARLIC-INFUSED OLIVE OIL

Makes 1 cup

> 1 cup pure olive oil
> 2 teaspoons minced garlic

Put the oil and garlic in a glass jar and let it stand in a cool dark place for 2 days.

Strain, discarding the garlic. Stored in a cool dark place, the oil will keep for 2 weeks. If you wish to extend its life, store the oil in the refrigerator, bringing it to room temperature before using.

GREEN OLIVE PESTO

Use this pesto in place of pesto sauce on Pizza alla Pesto (page 64) or on Roasted Pepper and Tomato Pizza (page 130).

Makes about 2 cups

> 1 cup sliced pitted green olives, rinsed and drained
> 2 cloves garlic, peeled
> ½ cup freshly grated Parmesan cheese
> ¼ cup pine nuts
> Salt and freshly ground black pepper to taste
> ½ cup olive oil

Put all the ingredients except the olive oil in the bowl of a food processor and process for 30 seconds. With the machine running, drizzle the oil through the feed tube and process until a smooth paste is formed. Add salt and freshly ground black pepper to taste.

GROUND TOMATOES

I said it in my first pizza cookbook, which I wrote in 1983, and I'll say it again: One of the best straight-from-the-can tomato puree products for use on pizza is 6 in 1 Ground Whole Tomatoes. It's packed by Escalon Packers in Escalon, California (209-838-7341).

This is a natural product with no added water or preservatives. Better yet, the product contains no citric acid, so the tomatoes have a naturally sweet flavor.

SUN-DRIED TOMATOES

I rarely purchase sun-dried tomatoes that are packed in oil, because they are too expensive. All the sun-dried tomatoes used in my cooking school are purchased dried and then processed as follows: Put the dried tomatoes and two peeled cloves of garlic in a pot of cold water. Bring the water to a boil, turn down the heat, and simmer for about 10 minutes, until the tomatoes are soft. Drain the liquid (you can strain it and save it as a flavoring for soups and sauces) and discard the garlic. When cool enough to handle, spread the tomatoes on paper toweling to dry, blotting excess moisture.

Now pack the tomatoes (not too tightly) in a jar with a tight-fitting lid. Fill the jar with olive oil just to cover the tomatoes. Store the jar in a cool place away from sunlight (in the refrigerator if the tomatoes are not going to be used within a month). Use the tomatoes directly from the jar in recipes that call for sun-dried tomatoes. Add olive oil to cover tomatoes as they are used or a mold will develop. Also, the olive oil works great for cooking or in salad dressing.

To increase the garlic flavor, pack two or three whole cloves of garlic in with the oil and tomatoes. Remove the garlic and discard it after no more than 6 days.

PEPPERS

How to Roast and Peel Red Peppers

While the jarred peppers are perfectly acceptable, you might enjoy roasting your own, especially in late summer, when the prices are low.

Wash each pepper by holding it under warm running water. Push the stem end of the pepper into the pepper and then pull it out intact and discard. Cut the pepper in half lengthwise and remove the seeds. Push down hard with your palm to flatten each half. Place the pepper halves on a baking sheet and put the pan under a preheated broiler about 3 to 4 inches from the heat. When the skin on the peppers chars and turns black, about 7 minutes, remove the peppers from the oven, put them in a metal bowl, and cover the bowl tightly with plastic wrap. This steaming will make it easier to remove the charred skin later. After about 30 minutes and up to an hour, remove the peppers from the bowl and peel and scrape off the skin.

The peppers can now be used in various recipes or placed in a jar with olive oil to cover and stored in a cool dark place for up to a month. If you're planning to use the peppers within 3 to 4 days, simply put them in a covered bowl in the refrigerator.

GARLIC

GARLIC CONFIT

Use this confit of garlic to spread over a pizza crust when making, for example, the Pizza Potato Pie on page 79.

Makes about ½ cup

> 6 large cloves garlic, peeled
> ½ cup olive oil

In a small saucepan, combine the garlic and olive oil. Bring to a simmer and cook over medium heat for 15–20 minutes or until the garlic is tender. Cool the mixture and transfer it to a clean glass jar with a tight-fitting lid. Kept covered and chilled, the garlic confit will keep for 6 months.

PIZZA POINTER

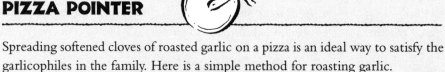

Spreading softened cloves of roasted garlic on a pizza is an ideal way to satisfy the garlicophiles in the family. Here is a simple method for roasting garlic.

Preheat the oven to 375°F. Remove the papery outer skin covering the head of garlic, but do not separate the cloves. Slice off about ½ inch of the top of the garlic head to expose the cloves. Place the garlic on a large square of aluminum foil and drizzle 1 teaspoon extra-virgin olive oil over the garlic. Fold the foil up around the garlic to enclose it completely. Bake for 1 hour or until soft (the exposed end of the clove can be pierced easily with the tip of a paring knife). Remove the garlic from the oven and, when cool enough to handle, separate the cloves and squeeze the garlic onto a pizza crust or over a baked pizza. One small head (a clove is one section; a head is the whole thing) of garlic (about 2 ounces) is sufficient for a 14-inch pizza.

Chapter 6

ITALY—THE GRAND TOUR

ITALIAN BAKERY PIZZA

In the early 1900s small Italian bakeries were commonplace in many northeastern states and across to the Midwest. Bread was the principal product of these bakeries, but pizza was a close second. This was pizza made in large rectangular pans—thicker and breadier than the style of pizzas today—with simple toppings, often nothing more than a puree of tomatoes, seasonings, and grated Parmesan or Romano cheese. Usually it was cut into squares and sold by the piece, but bakeries would frequently sell the entire pan (or several pans) for an event such as a wedding. Here is the pizza, as I remember it, that was made at the Italian bakery next door to our family home some fifty years ago. If you don't have a jelly-roll or similar pan, simply form the crust on a cookie sheet.

Makes one 12- by 15-inch pizza

> *1 recipe Pat's Favorite Pizza Dough in a single ball (page 23)*
> *1½ cups Herbed Tomato Sauce (page 37)*
> *½ cup freshly grated Romano or Parmesan cheese*
> *¼ pound mozzarella cheese, shredded (about 1 cup)*
> *2 tablespoons extra-virgin olive oil*

After the dough has doubled in bulk, do not punch it down. Lift the dough gently out of the bowl by sliding your hand underneath it. Lightly rub a 12- by 15-inch jelly-roll pan or baking sheet with olive oil. Place the dough in the center of the pan and press and push the dough to the size of the pan (at first the dough might pull back, so let it rest for a few minutes and it will cooperate).

Spread the sauce evenly over the dough, leaving about a ½-inch border all around.

Sprinkle the Romano cheese evenly over the tomato sauce. Sprinkle on the mozzarella.

Bake the pizza in the lower third of a preheated 450°F oven for 15–18 minutes or until the crust is golden brown. Drizzle the olive oil over the pizza, cut it into squares, and serve. The pizza is as good at room temperature as it is hot.

OPTIONS

◆ For a thicker, breadier crust, let the dough rise in the pan for 45 minutes before adding the toppings.

◆ Sausage was not used very often on Italian bakery pizza, but if you wish, sauté ¾ pound Italian sausage (casing removed) until it is just cooked through, breaking it into small chunks with a wooden spoon. Add the sausage topping *before* the cheeses.

SFINCIUNI

In Palmero, Sicily, pizza also goes by the name *sfinciuni*. The nuns of San Vito in Palermo are credited as the first to make this style of "pizza pie."

Of course, as it goes in Italy, every region has its own ideas, so in the north of Italy, in Emilia-Romagna, a similar "pizza" goes by the name *erbazzone*. The main idea is that the filling can be varied to taste. In some parts of Italy, for example, mortadella becomes a part of the filling.

This is a great pizza (aka torta) to make ahead and take on a picnic or outing. A few thin slices go a long way.

Makes one 9-inch sfinciuni

1 tablespoon olive oil

½ cup chopped onion

½ pound ground round

3 tablespoons chopped flat-leaf parsley

4 cups tightly packed fresh spinach leaves with no thick stems, washed and dried
    (about ½ pound)

¾ pound mozzarella cheese, shredded (about 3 cups)

½ cup freshly grated Parmesan cheese

⅛ teaspoon freshly ground black pepper

⅛ teaspoon salt

3 large eggs, lightly beaten

1 ball of Basic Pizza Dough II (page 25)

1 large egg, beaten with 2 teaspoons cold water

In a large skillet or sauté pan, warm the oil over medium heat for 1 minute. Add the onion, ground round, and parsley. Cook and stir for 3 minutes or until the meat has no trace of red. Drain off any excess grease. Set aside to cool for 10 minutes.

Coarsely chop the spinach and place it in a large mixing bowl. Add the mozzarella, Parmesan, pepper, and salt. Combine well, using your hands.

Add the reserved meat mixture to the spinach mixture. Add the 3 eggs. Using two large spoons, gently toss the mixture to combine. Set aside while you roll out the dough.

Lightly oil a 9-inch round cake pan. Cut a third of the dough off the dough ball and set it aside, covered. On a lightly floured surface, roll the remaining piece of dough into a circle about 11 inches in diameter so that when the dough is pushed into the pan it overhangs the sides by about ½ inch.

Place the filling in the pan, pushing it down gently with your hand to smooth the top.

On a lightly floured surface, roll the second piece of dough into a circle about 10 inches in diameter. Place the dough over the filling. Press the edges of the two layers of dough together with your fingers and roll the dough, tucking it inside the pan, as you would for a two-crust pie. With a sharp knife, cut a ½-inch slit in the middle of the top crust to allow the steam to escape. Brush the top crust, including the border, with the egg wash (you will use only a portion of the egg wash).

Bake the sfinciuni in the lower third of a preheated 425°F oven for 20–25 minutes, until the crust is golden brown. Let the sfinciuni sit for at least 30 minutes before cutting and serving. It is best served warm or at room temperature.

Pizza Trivia

In his book *The Food of Italy,* Waverley Root says, "Pizza basically means a pie, and can be applied to any flat round bakery product; but it is generally understood to mean the familiar circular tart. It is the direct descendant of the ancient Roman breakfast, 'bread with a relish.'"

PIZZA MARGHERITA

This is a classic Neapolitan pizza, the pizza that in 1889 first saw the light of cheese (see "Introduction: A Slice of History"). Undoubtedly the cheese used was the luxurious snow-white cheese made from the milk of the water buffalo—mozzarella di bufala. Because of its short shelf life, mozzarella di bufala is hard to find in this country, so the substitution of fresh mozzarella will do just fine. And if fresh mozzarella is not available, use regular mozzarella.

Makes one 14-inch pizza

> *1 recipe Basic Pizza Dough II (page 25)*
> *1 tablespoon extra-virgin olive oil*
> *1 cup chopped canned Italian-style plum tomatoes with as little juice as possible*
> *½ cup loosely packed torn fresh basil leaves*
> *6 ounces fresh mozzarella cheese (about 1 cup), sliced thin or chopped coarse*

With your fingers, press and form a ½-inch border around the crust. Brush or rub the crust with the olive oil.

Spread the tomatoes evenly over the crust up to the border. Sprinkle half the basil leaves evenly over the tomatoes. Arrange the fresh mozzarella over the tomatoes so that some of the tomatoes can be seen.

Bake the pizza on the bottom rack of a preheated 500°F oven for 10 minutes or until the crust is brown. Sprinkle on the remaining basil leaves as soon as the pizza comes out of the oven.

PIZZA NAPOLETANA

The fragrant and delicious flavors of true Neapolitan pizza are evident in every bite. Use the classic canned San Marzano tomatoes from Naples for an authentic touch. The final fillip that makes this pizza sing with flavor is a drizzle of fruity extra-virgin olive oil when the pizza comes out of the oven just before it is served. If you are a true garlic lover, use Garlic-Infused Olive Oil (page 47) in place of the regular olive oil.

Makes two 8- to 9-inch pizzas

> 1 recipe Basic Pizza Dough II (page 25), divided into 2 equal balls
> 1 28-ounce can Italian-style plum tomatoes (San Marzano if available), drained
>   thoroughly, crushed by hand in the can, and drained again
> 2 large cloves garlic, finely chopped
> ¼ pound mozzarella cheese, shredded (about 1 cup)
> 1 teaspoon dried oregano, crumbled
> 2 teaspoons extra-virgin olive oil

Stretch or roll each ball of dough into a circle about 9 inches in diameter. With your fingers, press and form a ½-inch border around the dough.

Spread an equal amount of the tomatoes over each pizza crust up to the border. Sprinkle half the garlic evenly over each pizza. Arrange evenly an equal amount of cheese over each pizza. Sprinkle an equal amount of oregano over each pizza.

Bake the pizzas on the bottom rack of a preheated 500°F oven for 8–10 minutes or until the crust is golden brown and the cheese has developed brown speckles.

As soon as the pizza comes out of the oven, just before serving, drizzle 1 teaspoon of olive oil over each pizza.

PIZZA RUSTICA

This two-crust pizza is an Italian Easter tradition, and just about every region of Italy has its own version. My mother never failed to make a number of these delicious Easter pies the day before Easter. The pizza keeps beautifully refrigerated, so we were still snacking on slices a week after Easter. One or two thin slices go a long way.

Makes one 10-inch pizza

DOUGH

2¼ cups unbleached all-purpose flour
¼ teaspoon freshly ground black pepper
¼ cup vegetable oil
⅓ cup water
2 large eggs

In a large mixing bowl, combine the flour and pepper and make a well in the center.

In a glass measuring cup, combine the oil and water. Beat in the eggs.

Pour the egg mixture into the flour well. Using a fork, and working from the inside of the well, combine the ingredients. Form the dough into a ball with your hands and knead gently for about 2 minutes. Let the dough rest, covered, while you prepare the filling.

FILLING

8 large eggs
1 teaspoon salt
1 pound or 1 15-ounce carton ricotta cheese
1 cup freshly grated Parmesan cheese
½ pound prosciutto, diced
1 pound provolone cheese, diced
1 egg, beaten with 1 tablespoon water

In a large mixing bowl, lightly beat the 8 eggs. Add the remaining ingredients except the egg and water and combine well. Set aside.

Divide the dough into two pieces. On a lightly floured surface, roll each piece of dough into a 15-inch circle. Fit one piece of dough into a 9-inch springform pan.

Pour the filling into the pan and smooth the top. Place the second piece of dough over the filling. Seal and crimp the edges.

Brush the top layer of dough generously with the egg wash and bake the pizza in a preheated 375°F oven for 1 hour, until the top is golden brown. Let the pizza cool for 1 hour. Carefully release the sides of the pan and gently remove the pizza from the pan. Place on large plate and refrigerate for 2 hours or overnight. Slice into wedges and serve at room temperature or slightly chilled.

PIZZA RIBOLLITA

Ribollita in its truest form is a hearty Tuscan bean soup. Here I've taken the idea—and many of its earthy flavors—into the domain of pizza. Don't look for a tomato sauce; there isn't one. This is a filling and hearty pizza with a great chew. Should there be leftovers, the pizza reheats nicely.

Makes one 13- to 14-inch pizza

> 1 pound redskin potatoes, peeled and cut into small cubes (about 2 cups)
>
> 1 15-ounce can cannellini, drained and rinsed
>
> 2 cloves garlic, finely chopped
>
> 1 ¼-pound piece of prosciutto about ¼ inch thick, trimmed of fat and
>   cut into small cubes
>
> ½ cup chopped onion
>
> 2 teaspoons chopped fresh rosemary or ½ teaspoon dried
>
> 2 teaspoons chopped fresh thyme or ½ teaspoon dried
>
> ¼ teaspoon hot red pepper flakes
>
> 2 tablespoons freshly grated Parmesan cheese
>
> 3 tablespoons extra-virgin olive oil
>
> 1 pizza shell from Pat's Favorite Pizza Dough (page 23)
>
> 10 ounces mozzarella cheese, shredded (about 2½ cups)

Cook the potatoes in boiling salted water for 8–9 minutes or until barely tender. Cool for 5 minutes.

In a large mixing bowl, combine the cooked potatoes, beans, garlic, prosciutto, and onion. Add the rosemary, thyme, red pepper flakes, and Parmesan cheese. Drizzle in the olive oil and mix gently to combine the ingredients well. (The recipe can be made up to this point and held for several hours or overnight, refrigerated.)

With your fingers, press and form a ½-inch border around the crust.

Spread half of the cheese evenly over the crust. Spread the bean mixture evenly over the cheese. Sprinkle on the remaining cheese.

Bake the pizza on the bottom rack of a preheated 500°F oven for 10–12 minutes or until the crust is golden brown and the cheese is just beginning to brown.

OPTIONS

A classic ribollita requires that a sauce be drizzled into the soup just at the end. It works nicely on the pizza too. Should you choose to go all the way, here is the recipe:

> ¼ cup extra-virgin olive oil
> 2 cloves garlic, crushed
> 1 small sprig fresh rosemary, chopped
> 1 sprig fresh thyme, chopped, or ½ teaspoon dried
> ½ teaspoon hot red pepper flakes or ½ teaspoon minced fresh chilies

Place all the ingredients in a small skillet or saucepan and cook over medium heat for 3 minutes. Strain the sauce into a heatproof measuring cup.

Drizzle a tablespoon or more over the pizza when it comes out of the oven.

Pizza Party

Have a pizza party with Pizza Ribollita (page 60) and Pizza Marengo (page 62), two lusty, chunky, chewy, flavorful pizzas that answer the call of the hungry.

PIZZA MARENGO

Chicken Marengo was created by Napoléon's cook, Dundand, at Marengo, a small town in the Piedmont region of Italy. Napoléon had just defeated the Austrians (June 14, 1800) and, so the story goes, was famished. Dundand, however, had very little to work with, the commissary having been left behind because Napoléon was in hot pursuit. So he foraged around and came up with some chicken, tomatoes, garlic, and crayfish—some fried eggs got into the picture somewhere, too.

Well, the contemporary version of chicken (and veal) Marengo does not include either crayfish or eggs but rather onions, mushrooms, and olives. Here it is in pizza form—and quite delicious at that.

Makes one 13- to 14-inch pizza

> 2 tablespoons extra-virgin olive oil
> ¾ pound skinless, boneless chicken breast, cut into 1-inch cubes
> 1 large (about ½ pound) green bell pepper, chopped (about 1½ cups)
> ½ cup chopped onion
> 2 cloves garlic, crushed
> ½ pound mushrooms, sliced (about 2½ cups tightly packed)
> Salt and freshly ground black pepper to taste
> 12 oil-cured or brine-cured olives, pitted and chopped
> 1 pizza shell from Pat's Favorite Pizza Dough (page 23)
> ¾ cup Herbed Tomato Sauce (page 37)
> ½ pound scamorza or mozzarella cheese, shredded (about 2 cups)

In a large skillet or sauté pan, warm the oil over medium heat for 1 minute. Add the chicken, green pepper, onion, and garlic. Cook and stir for about 8 minutes or until the chicken is cooked through and the peppers begin to soften. Add the mushrooms and cook for 2 minutes. Add salt and pepper to taste. Fold in the olives. (The recipe can be made up to this point and held for several hours or overnight, refrigerated.)

With your fingers, press and form a ½-inch border around the crust.

Spread the sauce evenly over the crust. Spread the chicken mixture evenly over the tomatoes. Sprinkle on the shredded cheese.

Bake the pizza on the bottom rack of a preheated 500°F oven for 8–10 minutes or until the crust is golden brown.

PIZZA GIAMBOTTA

One of the most flavorful dishes in the Italian repertoire is a giambotta or mixture of Italian sausage, sweet peppers, and onions. In this pizza version I have added tomato sauce and cheese. This is a hearty and substantial pizza, one that makes a great centerpiece for a pizza party.

Makes two 13- to 14-inch pizzas

> *¾ pound sweet Italian sausage in casing*
>
> *2 tablespoons olive oil*
>
> *1 cup chopped onion*
>
> *1 recipe Pat's Favorite Pizza Dough (page 23)*
>
> *1½ cups tomato puree or Herbed Tomato Sauce (page 37)*
>
> *1 pound mozzarella cheese, shredded (about 4 cups)*
>
> *1 medium red bell pepper, roasted, peeled, and chopped (page 48)*
>
> *1 medium green bell pepper, roasted, peeled, and chopped (page 48)*
>
> *1 teaspoon dried oregano, crumbled*

In a large skillet or over a hot grill, cook the sausages in the olive oil in their casing until cooked through, about 10 minutes. Remove the sausages from the pan and, when cool enough to handle, cut them into ½-inch-thick coins.

To the pan in which the sausage was cooked, add the onion and cook over medium heat for 2 minutes to soften. Reserve. (The recipe can be made up to this point and held for up to 2 hours or overnight.)

With your fingers, press and form a ½-inch border around each crust.

Spread half of the tomato puree over each pizza up to the border. Spread half of the onion over each pizza. Arrange half of the sausage coins evenly over each pizza. Sprinkle ½ pound (2 cups) of the shredded cheese over each pizza. Arrange half of the red and green peppers over each pizza, pressing them gently into the cheese. Sprinkle ½ teaspoon oregano over each pizza.

Bake the pizzas on the bottom rack of a preheated 500°F oven for 10 minutes or until the crust is golden brown and the cheese is melted and speckled brown.

PIZZA ALLA PESTO

In Genoa, in the Ligurian region of Italy, the smell of fresh basil hangs fragrant in the air. Basil grows merrily in window boxes, clay pots, cans—you name it. The people of Genoa love their basil and use it in cooking in every way imaginable. Pesto, that sublime combination of fresh basil, garlic, olive oil, pine nuts, and grated cheeses, is the most popular Genovese contribution to the culinary world. This pizza is a variation of the famous pasta dish pesto alla Genovese, in which trenette pasta mingles deliciously with pesto sauce, potatoes, and string beans. I use sun-dried tomatoes instead of string beans and a mellow mozzarella to tune up the balance of flavors.

You will have more pesto sauce than you can use, so freeze the balance or have it with pasta another day. The sauce will keep in the refrigerator, covered, for 3–4 days.

Makes one 14-inch pizza

PESTO SAUCE

Makes 1½–2 cups

2 cups loosely packed fresh basil leaves
2 cloves garlic, peeled
2 tablespoons freshly grated Parmesan cheese
2 tablespoons grated Romano cheese
¼ cup pine nuts
½ cup plus 1 tablespoon extra-virgin olive oil
Salt and freshly ground black pepper to taste

Place the basil, reserving 10–12 leaves for garnish, garlic, cheeses, and pine nuts in a food processor fitted with the steel blade. Pulse the machine 10–12 times or until the ingredients are combined thoroughly. With the motor running, slowly add the olive oil. Process until smooth. Season with salt and pepper. (The sauce can be made ahead and kept in the refrigerator, covered, for 3–4 days.)

1½ pounds new potatoes, peeled and cut into small cubes
1 recipe Basic Pizza Dough II (page 25)
¼ cup pesto sauce
¼ cup chopped oil-packed sun-dried tomatoes (page 48)
½ pound mozzarella, shredded (about 2 cups)
10–12 fresh basil leaves, torn into small pieces

Place the potatoes in a saucepan of boiling salted water. Cook until barely tender, 8–9 minutes. Drain and reserve.

With your fingers, press and form a ½-inch border around the crust.

Spread the pesto sauce evenly over the pizza crust up to the border. Sprinkle on the sun-dried tomatoes. Arrange the potatoes evenly over the crust. Sprinkle on the mozzarella.

Bake the pizza on the bottom rack of a preheated 500°F oven for 8–10 minutes or until the crust is golden brown. Just before serving, sprinkle the fresh basil leaves over the cheese.

Pizza Party Pizzas

These recipes yield multiple pizzas, perfect for throwing a pizza party!

Pizza Giambotta (page 63)
Pizza Provolone with Italian Sausage (page 70)
Maria's Sausage Pizza (page 72)
Four-Cheese Veggie Pizza (page 129)

TORTA PASQUALINA

Every region of Italy has a torta of some kind, and except for the person making the torta the filling is an unknown entity until the torta is cut and the first slice is served. This version is typical of tortas made during the Easter season.

Makes one 9-inch torta

DOUGH

2¼ cups unbleached all-purpose flour

¾ teaspoon salt

1 teaspoon freshly ground black pepper

½ cup warm water (105–115°F)

½ cup olive oil

In a large bowl, combine the flour, salt, pepper, water, and olive oil until a dough is formed, adding 1–2 tablespoons of flour if necessary to make a firm, nonsticky dough. Shape the dough into a ball and chill it, covered, while you make the filling.

FILLING

2 tablespoons olive oil

2 cloves garlic, minced

¼ cup chopped onion

*½ pound fresh spinach (about 6 cups) leaves with no thick stems, washed,
    patted dry, and chopped coarse*

*1 9-ounce package frozen artichoke hearts, cooked according to package directions,
    each heart cut in half*

1 cup ricotta cheese

½ cup freshly grated Parmesan cheese

3 large eggs, lightly beaten

¼ teaspoon salt

⅛ teaspoon freshly ground black pepper

1 egg, beaten with 2 tablespoons water

In a deep skillet or sauté pan over medium-high heat, warm the oil for 1 minute. Add the garlic, onion, and spinach. Sauté the mixture until the spinach wilts down and is tender, about 5 minutes. Set aside.

In a large bowl, combine the artichokes, ricotta, Parmesan, eggs, salt, and pepper.

Divide the dough in half and roll each half on a lightly floured surface to a thickness of about $\frac{1}{16}$ inch. Fit one piece of dough into a 10-inch deep-dish pizza pan or cake pan.

Spread the filling into the pan, leveling the top with the back of a spoon. Layer the spinach mixture evenly over the filling.

Top the filling with the remaining piece of dough and roll, press, and seal the edges. Brush the top crust with the egg wash.

Bake the torta in the bottom third of a preheated 375°F oven for 50 minutes or until the crust is golden brown. Let cool slightly before cutting and serving.

Pizza Trivia

The plural of *pizza* is *pizze*.
The plural of *pizzeria* is *pizzerie*.

PIZZA LIGURIA

Pizza Liguria takes us to the countryside near Genoa, where we enjoy a pizza fragrant with olives and anchovies.

Makes one 12-inch pizza

> *1 28-ounce can Italian-style plum tomatoes, drained*
> *2 tablespoons chopped onion*
> *2 small cloves garlic, minced*
> *2 tablespoons freshly grated Parmesan cheese*
> *1 ball of Beer Crust dough (page 27)*
> *6 ounces mozzarella cheese, shredded (about 1½ cups)*
> *15–16 oil-cured olives, pitted and cut in half*
> *6–8 anchovy fillets*

Empty the drained tomatoes into a mixing bowl and crush them with your hands. Drain excess juice, crush some more, and drain again.

Add the onion, garlic, and Parmesan cheese to the tomatoes and combine well.

Roll the dough into a 12-inch circle. With your fingers, press and form a ½-inch border around the crust.

Spread the tomato mixture evenly over the crust up to the border. Sprinkle the mozzarella over the tomatoes. Arrange the olives and anchovy fillets decoratively on the cheese.

Bake the pizza in a preheated 500°F oven for 10 minutes or until the crust is golden brown.

PIZZA TREVISO

Treviso is a 10-minute train ride from Venice. Radicchio (known as *red chicory* in Italy) is enjoyed either cooked or raw in the Veneto region.

Makes one 12-inch pizza

> 1 ball of Beer Crust dough (page 27)
> 2 medium fresh tomatoes, sliced (about 10 slices)
> 1 tablespoon chopped fresh oregano or ½ teaspoon dried, crumbled
> 1½ cups coarsely chopped radicchio
> 1 cup sliced mushrooms
> ¼ pound Asiago or mozzarella cheese, shredded (about 1 cup)

Roll the dough into a 12-inch circle. With your fingers, press and form a ½-inch border around the crust.

Arrange the sliced tomatoes evenly over the crust up to the border. Sprinkle on the oregano. Sprinkle the radicchio evenly over the tomatoes. Arrange the mushrooms over the radicchio. Sprinkle on the cheese.

Bake the pizza on the bottom rack of a preheated 500°F oven for 10 minutes or until the crust is golden brown.

Pizza Party

Have a pizza party that features an Italian coast-to-coast duet of pizzas: Pizza Liguria (page 68) and Pizza Treviso (above).

PIZZA PROVOLONE
WITH ITALIAN SAUSAGE

Semolina flour adds not only a pleasant crunch to the crust but a buttery consistency as well, one that works nicely with the assertive flavor of the provolone cheese. If you choose not to make all three pizzas, freeze the dough that you don't use.

Makes three 12- to 13-inch pizzas

DOUGH

2 ¼-ounce envelopes (5 teaspoons) active dry yeast
½ cup warm water (105–115°F)
1 teaspoon sugar
3 tablespoons vegetable oil
3¼ cups unbleached all-purpose flour
1 cup semolina flour
2 teaspoons salt
1 cup warm water (105–115°F)

In a large mixing bowl or the bowl of a stand mixer, dissolve the yeast in ½ cup warm water. Add the sugar and combine well. Let stand for 5 minutes.

Add the oil to the yeast mixture and stir to combine. Add the flour, semolina, salt, and 1 cup water.

Combine, mix, and knead the dough for about 6 minutes, until the dough is smooth and elastic. If you're using a stand mixer fitted with a dough hook, knead for 4–5 minutes at high speed. Dust lightly with additional flour if needed. The dough should feel moist on the surface but should not stick to your hand.

Divide the dough into three equal balls. Place the balls of dough on a lightly floured baking sheet, spacing them about 3 inches apart. Flatten the tops with your palm. Dust the tops lightly with flour. Cover with plastic wrap.

Let the dough rise for 1–1½ hours or until doubled in bulk (at this point any dough not being used should be punched down, balled tightly, put into a lightly floured plastic bag, and frozen for later use).

Flatten each piece of dough with your palm and push it by hand or roll it out on a lightly floured surface. Fit each piece of dough into a lightly oiled 12-inch round pizza pan. If you're using a baking stone, transfer the dough to a lightly floured pizza peel. Cover any of the dough not being baked at once with plastic wrap.

TOPPING

¾ *pound sweet Italian sausage, casing removed*

3 cups canned all-purpose ground tomatoes or tomato puree

2 teaspoons dried oregano, crumbled

2 teaspoons dried basil, crumbled

2 cloves garlic, pressed

1 pound shredded provolone cheese (about 4 cups)

In a skillet, cook the sausage over medium heat, stirring and breaking up the lumps, just until it is no longer pink, about 4 minutes. Remove the skillet from the heat and drain off any excess fat.

Season the tomatoes with the oregano, basil, and garlic.

Just before baking, top each pizza crust with equal amounts of tomatoes, followed by cheese and then sausage, pushing the sausage down into the cheese.

Bake the pizzas on the bottom rack of a preheated 500°F oven for 10–12 minutes, until the crust is golden brown and the cheese just starts to develop brown speckles.

MARIA'S SAUSAGE PIZZA

Though our family home was smack next door to an Italian bakery, a bakery with dough ready to go to make pizza, my mother felt the need to make her own dough for pizza at least once a week, so just about every Saturday of the year she would make pizza for my three brothers and me.

To this day the taste of that pizza lingers on my taste buds. This is as close as I can get to duplicating the delicious pizza my mother served every Saturday.

Makes two 14- to 15-inch pizzas

> *1 tablespoon olive oil*
> *2 cloves garlic, sliced thin*
> *1½ pounds sweet Italian sausage, casing removed*
> *1½ teaspoons fennel seed*
> *2 28-ounce cans Italian-style plum tomatoes, drained and chopped*
> *1 teaspoon dried oregano, crumbled*
> *Salt to taste*
> *1 recipe Friday Night Pizza Dough (page 28)*
> *¼ cup torn fresh basil leaves or 2 teaspoons dried, crumbled*
> *¼ cup freshly grated Parmesan cheese*
> *1 pound mozzarella cheese, shredded (about 4 cups)*

In a sauté pan over medium heat, warm the olive oil for 1 minute. Sauté the garlic until golden and discard. Add the sausage and fennel to the skillet; sauté until the sausage is just cooked through, stirring often, about 4 minutes.

Add the drained tomatoes to the pan. Break up the tomatoes with the edge of a wooden spoon. Add the oregano. Bring the mixture to a boil and cook over moderate heat, stirring occasionally, for 20–25 minutes or until the sauce is thickened and reduced to about 2½ cups. Add salt to taste. Cool the sauce for at least 30 minutes before using. The sauce can be kept for 1 week, covered and refrigerated.

With your fingers, press and form a ½-inch border around each crust.

Divide the sauce between the two pizza crusts, spreading it evenly up to the border. Divide the fresh basil evenly between the pizzas. Divide the Parmesan between the pizzas, sprinkling it evenly over the tomatoes. Divide the mozzarella evenly between the pizzas.

Bake the pizzas on the bottom rack of a preheated 500°F oven for 10–12 minutes or until the crust is golden brown.

Chapter 7

AROUND THE MEDITERRANEAN

MAGNIFICENT GREEK PIZZA

The flavors of Greece and the Mediterranean stand out most vividly in this pizza. However, to get the real bloom of Greek flavor you should use brine-cured Greek olives such as Atalanti (aka Royal), Kalamata, or Amfissa. An alternative would be brine-cured Greek-style olives from California.

Makes one 14-inch pizza

1 10-ounce package fresh spinach
¼ cup water
2 tablespoons extra-virgin olive oil
2 cloves garlic, minced
¼ cup finely chopped red onion
⅛ teaspoon freshly ground black pepper
Salt to taste
1 recipe Basic Pizza Dough II (page 25)
½ cup sliced pitted brine-cured green olives
½ cup sliced pitted brine-cured black olives
¼ pound feta cheese, crumbled (about 1 cup)

Wash the spinach and pull off the thicker stems. Put the water and spinach in a large pot and cook over medium-high heat, covered, until the spinach wilts, about 6 minutes. Drain the excess liquid from the pan. With the cover off, cook and stir the spinach for 2 minutes to allow some of the moisture to evaporate.

Add the olive oil, garlic, onion, and pepper to the spinach. Cook and stir over medium heat for 4 minutes. Add salt to taste. Set aside.

With your fingers, press and form a ½-inch border around the crust.

Spread the spinach mixture evenly over the crust up to the border. Sprinkle the olives evenly over the spinach. Sprinkle the feta cheese evenly over the pizza.

Bake the pizza on the bottom rack of a preheated 500°F oven for 10–12 minutes or until the crust is golden brown.

PIZZA ATTSA NICE

This is my version of a pissaladière, the famous onion pizza that is so highly favored in Nice and along the French Riviera. I added sun-dried tomatoes and left off the anchovies, but feel free to add the anchovies (in a spoke-like fashion).

Makes one 13- to 14-inch pizza

> 2 large onions, julienned (about 3½ cups)
> 2 small cloves garlic, minced
> 5 tablespoons extra-virgin olive oil
> 1 teaspoon dried thyme, crumbled
> 1 teaspoon dried tarragon, crumbled
> ¼ cup chopped flat-leaf parsley
> ½ cup low-salt chicken broth
> 1 recipe Basic Pizza Dough II (page 25)
> ½ cup chopped oil-packed sun-dried tomatoes (page 48)
> 16 Niçoise or other brine-cured olives, pitted

In a large skillet over medium-high heat, sauté the onions and garlic in 3 tablespoons of the olive oil for 3 minutes, stirring frequently. Add the thyme, tarragon, parsley, and chicken broth. Cook and stir for about 4 minutes or until the onions are soft and limp and all of the chicken broth has evaporated. Set aside for about 5 minutes to cool slightly.

With your fingers, press and form a ½-inch border around the crust.

Spread the onion mixture evenly over the pizza shell up to the border. Arrange the sun-dried tomatoes and olives over the onions.

Bake the pizza on the bottom rack of a preheated 500°F oven for 10 minutes or until the crust is brown. Drizzle the remaining olive oil evenly over the pizza just before serving. Cut and serve at once.

PIZZA POMODORO FRESCA

Fresh tomatoes that are almost dead-ripe are the sauce that makes this pizza sing with flavor. Feel free to vary the flavor by adding some chopped fresh basil to taste, which, along with the olives, gives these pizzas a true Mediterranean flavor.

Makes two 8- to 9-inch pizzas

> 1 recipe Basic Pizza Dough II (page 25), divided into 2 equal pieces
> 2 large tomatoes (each about 5 ounces), sliced ⅛ inch thick
> 2 teaspoons extra-virgin olive oil
> 1 teaspoon dried oregano, crumbled
> ¼ pound mozzarella cheese, cubed (about 1 cup)
> 16 oil-cured olives, pitted
> 4 teaspoons freshly grated Parmesan cheese

Stretch or roll each ball of dough into a circle about 9 inches in diameter. With your fingers, press and form a half-inch border around the crust.

Arrange the tomato slices on each pizza shell up to the border. Drizzle 1 teaspoon of the olive oil evenly over the tomatoes on each pizza. Divide the remaining ingredients evenly between the two pizzas.

Bake the pizzas one at a time—or put both pizza crusts on a baking sheet—on the bottom rack of a preheated 500°F oven for 8–10 minutes or until the crust is golden brown and the cheese starts to take on brown speckles.

SPINACH PIZZA WITH PROVOLONE AND MUSHROOMS

One of my great loves is spinach sautéed with oil and garlic. In this version of spinach pizza I combine that love with another fancy I have—mushrooms. No tomatoes on this one; let the spinach and cheese flavors come through on their own.

Makes one 14-inch pizza

> 1 10-ounce package fresh spinach
> ¼ cup water
> 3 tablespoons olive oil
> 2 cloves garlic, minced
> 1 cup sliced mushrooms
> Salt and freshly ground black pepper to taste
> 1 recipe Basic Pizza Dough II (page 25)
> 2 tablespoons Garlic-Infused Olive Oil (page 47)
> ¼ cup freshly grated Parmesan cheese
> ½ pound provolone, shredded (about 2 cups)

Wash the spinach and remove the thick stems. Place the spinach and water in a deep saucepan or sauté pan over low heat. Cover the pan and cook until the spinach wilts into the pan, about 4 minutes. Drain excess water from the pan. Put the pan back on the burner and raise the heat to medium-high.

Add the olive oil, garlic, and mushrooms. Cook and stir for 3–4 minutes or until the mushrooms just begin to soften. Add salt and pepper to taste. Reserve and cool slightly. (The spinach can be prepared to this point and held for 2–3 hours.)

With your fingers, press and form a 1-inch border around the crust.

Brush the crust with the Garlic-Infused Olive Oil. Spread the spinach mixture over the crust up to the border. Sprinkle the Parmesan evenly over the spinach, followed by the provolone.

Bake the pizza on the bottom rack of a preheated 500°F oven for 10–12 minutes or until the crust is brown and the cheese begins to take on color.

PIZZA POTATO PIE

A classic French potato dish adapted for pizza. This pizza cries out for a good hit of garlic, so don't hold back if you're a garlic lover. The cheese goes on the crust, and the potatoes go over the cheese—a reverse of the usual pizza-topping procedure. The potatoes can be prepared 3–4 hours ahead, so the final assembly and baking take very little time.

Makes one 14-inch pizza

> *2 pounds russet baking potatoes, peeled and placed in a saucepan of cold water to cover*
> *2 tablespoons unsalted butter*
> *1 tablespoon olive oil*
> *1 tablespoon minced fresh rosemary or 1 teaspoon dried, crumbled*
> *⅛ teaspoon freshly ground black pepper*
> *⅛ teaspoon salt*
> *1 recipe Basic Pizza Dough II (page 25)*
> *1 recipe Garlic Confit (page 49)*
> *¾ cup shredded Gruyère or mild cheddar cheese*
> *2 tablespoons Garlic-Infused Olive Oil (page 47)*
> *3 tablespoons freshly grated Parmesan cheese*

Place the saucepan with the potatoes and cold water over high heat and boil for about 25 minutes or until the potatoes are barely tender. Do not overcook, or they will not slice well and hold their shape. Drain the potatoes and, when cool enough to handle, slice them into rounds about ¼ inch thick.

In a 12- to 13-inch sauté pan or skillet, melt the butter with the oil over medium-high heat. When the butter starts to froth, place the potatoes in one layer in the pan (cook the potatoes in two batches if you don't have a large enough pan). Add the rosemary, pepper, and salt. Cook the potatoes until they turn golden brown and crispy on one side, about 6–7 minutes. Transfer the potatoes to a dinner plate and let cool for about 10 minutes.

With your fingers, press and form a ½-inch border around the pizza crust.

Rub and spread the Garlic Confit over the pizza crust. Sprinkle the Gruyère cheese evenly over the crust up to the border. Arrange the potatoes over the cheese, overlapping the slices if necessary. Brush the potatoes with the Garlic-Infused Olive Oil. Sprinkle the Parmesan evenly over the potatoes.

Bake the pizza on the bottom rack of a preheated 500°F oven for 10 minutes or until the crust is golden brown.

PIZZA WITH FRESH TOMATOES AND HAM
(Pan con Tomate, Jamón, y Queso)

In my journeys to Spain I fell in love with a first plate or tapa called *pan con tomate* (bread with tomato) that is common to most restaurants. In its classic form *pan con tomate* (*pa amb tomaquet* in Catalán) is simply grilled or toasted bread that has been rubbed with garlic and fresh tomatoes. It's delicious. Here is my pizza version of *pan con tomate* (also see Pizza on the Grill, page 19) with ham and cheese added to embrace more fully the flavors of Spain. If you can't get Manchego cheese, use white cheddar.

Makes one 14-inch pizza

> 1 recipe Basic Pizza Dough II (page 25)
> 1 tablespoon Garlic-Infused Olive Oil (page 47)
> ¾ pound dead-ripe fresh plum tomatoes, sliced lengthwise about ¼ inch thick
> 1 tablespoon chopped fresh oregano or ½ teaspoon dried, crumbled
> ¼ pound Spanish ham (jamón serrano) or imported prosciutto, sliced almost paper-thin
> ½ pound Manchego cheese, shredded (about 2 cups)

With your fingers, press and form a ½-inch border around the crust.

Brush the crust, including the border, with the Garlic-Infused Olive Oil. Arrange the sliced tomatoes evenly over the crust up to the border. Sprinkle the oregano over the tomatoes. Arrange the ham over the tomatoes and sprinkle the cheese evenly over the ham.

Bake the pizza on the bottom rack of a preheated 500°F oven for 10 minutes or until the pizza crust is golden brown.

LEEK AND SUN-DRIED TOMATO PIZZA

Leek, a member of the onion family, plays a subtle yet flavorful part in this simple yet tasty pizza. The main components—leeks, sun-dried tomatoes, and sauce—can be prepared well ahead. So once the dough is ready it's just a few short steps from start to eating enjoyment.

Makes one 12- to 13-inch pizza

> *1½ pounds leeks*
> *2 tablespoons extra-virgin olive oil*
> *1 recipe Basic Pizza Dough II (page 25)*
> *¾ cup Herbed Tomato Sauce (page 37)*
> *½ cup chopped oil-packed sun-dried tomatoes*
> *6 ounces Manchego or white cheddar cheese, shredded (about 2½ cups)*
> *¼ pound prosciutto, cut into ⅛-inch strips*

Trim the leeks, leaving on about 1 inch of the pale green stalk. Cut the leek lengthwise and wash thoroughly (soil lurks in the "leaves" of the bulb) in cold water. Chop the leeks crosswise. You should have about 2 cups.

In a sauté pan or skillet, sauté the leeks in the oil over medium-high heat for 3 to 4 minutes or until they just begin to soften. Reserve.

With your fingers, press and form a ½-inch border around the crust.

Spread the sauce evenly over the crust up to the border. Sprinkle on the sun-dried tomatoes, then the leeks, then the cheese, then the prosciutto.

Bake the pizza on the bottom rack of a preheated 500°F oven for 10 minutes or until the crust is golden brown.

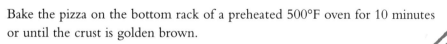

PANCETTA AND POTATO PIZZA

Makes one 13- to 14-inch pizza

> ¼ pound lean pancetta, chopped
> 1 shell from Pat's Favorite Pizza Dough (page 23)
> 2 tablespoons Garlic-Infused Olive Oil (page 47)
> 1 large redskin potato (about ¾ pound), peeled and sliced almost paper-thin
> ¼ cup chopped scallion, white part only
> ½ teaspoon dried rosemary, crumbled, or 2 teaspoons fresh, chopped
> ½ teaspoon dried thyme, crumbled, or 2 teaspoons fresh, chopped
> 2 teaspoons hot red pepper flakes
> 3 tablespoons freshly grated Parmesan cheese

In a small sauté pan over low heat, cook the pancetta until it renders most of its fat and starts to get crispy, about 7 minutes. Reserve in the pan.

With your fingers, press and form a 1-inch border around the crust.

Brush the crust with the Garlic-Infused Olive Oil. Arrange the potatoes over the crust up to the border, overlapping them if necessary. Sprinkle the scallions over the potatoes. Sprinkle on the rosemary, thyme, and red pepper flakes. Pour the reserved pancetta, including the fat in the pan, evenly over the pizza. Sprinkle the Parmesan evenly over the pizza.

Bake the pizza on the bottom rack of a preheated 500°F oven for 9–10 minutes or until the crust is brown and crispy.

Pizza Trivia

October is National Pizza Month.

Chapter 8

PIZZA ACROSS AMERICA

BARBECUE CHICKEN PIZZA

With but four basic ingredients, this pizza goes together fast—yet it's absolutely delicious. Simply by changing the brand of barbecue sauce you can spice it up or spice it down to taste.

Makes two 12-inch pizzas

> 3 tablespoons vegetable oil
> 2 whole skinless, boneless chicken breasts, cut into small cubes
> 1 recipe Beer Crust dough (page 27)
> 1 cup K.C. Masterpiece Original barbecue sauce
> 1 cup chopped red onion
> 1½ cups shredded smoked mozzarella

In a skillet over medium-high heat, warm the vegetable oil for 1 minute. Add the chicken. Stir and cook until the chicken is cooked through, about 4 minutes. Remove the chicken from the pan with a slotted spoon and reserve. (The chicken can be done a day ahead and refrigerated until ready to use.)

With your fingers, press and form a ½-inch border around each crust.

In a large bowl, toss the cooked chicken with the barbecue sauce to coat. Divide the chicken equally between the two pizza shells. Sprinkle ½ cup of the red onion evenly over each pizza. Sprinkle an equal portion of the cheese on each pizza.

Bake the pizza on the bottom rack of a preheated 500°F oven for 10 minutes or until the crust is brown and the cheese is melted and bubbly.

CHICKEN AND BLUE CHEESE PIZZA

This is the pizza for people who love the spicy flavor of Buffalo chicken wings paired with the tangy flavor of blue cheese. The toppings can be made well ahead, and once the dough is ready it is just a matter of adding the finishing touches and baking. For an extra treat, see "Options" for making a tasty focaccia or table bread with the remaining dough.

Makes one 12-inch pizza

> 1 pound skinless, boneless chicken breasts
> 3 tablespoons unsalted butter
> 3 tablespoons Louisiana hot sauce
> 1 tablespoon cider vinegar
> ½ cup sour cream
> ½ cup ricotta cheese
> ½ cup crumbled blue cheese
> 1 ball of Beer Crust dough (page 27)

Poach the chicken breasts in boiling water until cooked, about 15 minutes. Remove the chicken from the water and, when cool enough to handle, cut it into ½-inch-wide strips and then cut the strips in half crosswise. Put the chicken in a mixing bowl and reserve.

In a small saucepan, melt the butter over medium heat. Stir in the hot sauce and vinegar. Cook the sauce, simmering gently, for about 3 minutes.

Off the heat, add the chicken to the sauce and toss to coat. (The chicken can be prepared several hours ahead and held, refrigerated.)

In a mixing bowl or food processor, combine the sour cream, ricotta, and ¼ cup of the blue cheese. Beat or process until a smooth sauce is formed. (The sauce can be prepared several hours ahead or overnight and held, refrigerated.)

With your fingers, press and form a ½-inch border around the crust.

Spread the sauce evenly over the pizza up to the border. Arrange the chicken evenly over the sauce, pushing the pieces gently into the sauce with your fingers or the back of a spoon. Sprinkle the remaining blue cheese evenly over the pizza.

Bake the pizza on the bottom rack of a preheated 500°F oven for 8–10 minutes or until the crust is golden brown.

OPTIONS

Garlic Focaccia

Place the second ball of dough from the Beer Crust recipe on a lightly oiled flat pizza pan. Press the dough with your hands into a 10-inch circle. Push the tips of your fingers deep into the dough all over the surface. Brush the top of the dough with 2 tablespoons Garlic-Infused Olive Oil (page 47). Bake the focaccia in a preheated 450°F oven for 18–20 minutes, until the top is golden brown. Set the focaccia on a wire cooling rack. When cool, slice into strips and serve as a table bread. Freeze any leftovers.

FRIED TOMATO PIZZA
(Pizza Pomodori Fritti)

A perfect way to heighten the flavor of tomatoes and have your pizza, too. Don't use dead-ripe tomatoes; they'll fall apart during the frying. Firm, almost-ripe tomatoes are best, and green tomatoes work fine, too. The fried tomatoes by themselves make a delicious appetizer, so watch out for hungry eaters nearby if you don't want the tomatoes to disappear before you make the pizza.

Serve this one hot or at room temperature—make it ahead for a patio dinner or picnic. You must use semolina flour, or the recipe will not work.

Makes one 12-inch pizza

> *½ cup milk*
> *1 cup semolina flour*
> *3 tablespoons freshly grated Romano or Parmesan cheese*
> *⅛ teaspoon salt*
> *⅛ teaspoon freshly ground black pepper*
> *1 pound firm, medium-ripe slicing tomatoes, trimmed and sliced into rounds*
>   *about ½ inch thick (10–12 slices)*
> *Vegetable oil for frying*
> *1 large ball of Whole-Wheat Pizza Dough (page 30)*
> *12 large fresh basil leaves*
> *½ pound Asiago or fontina cheese, shredded (about 2 cups)*

Place the milk in a wide soup bowl or small mixing bowl and the semolina flour in another. Add the Romano, salt, and pepper to the semolina. Dip the tomato slices, one by one, in the milk and then the semolina, pressing the semolina lightly into the tomatoes. Arrange the tomatoes in a single layer on a square of aluminum foil.

In a saucepan wide enough to hold two tomato slices at a time, pour enough vegetable oil to measure about 1½ inches. Heat the oil until it registers about 375°F on a deep-frying thermometer. (If you don't have one, drop a cube of bread about 1 inch square into the oil. If the cube browns in about 1 minute, the oil temperature should be right.)

Fry the tomatoes two at a time for 30–45 seconds or until they turn golden brown. Remove the tomatoes with a slotted spoon and transfer them to a plate lined with two layers of paper toweling. (The tomatoes can be prepared several hours ahead and kept at room temperature.)

Roll or press the ball of dough into a 13-inch circle. With your fingers, press and form a ½-inch border around the crust.

Arrange the fried tomatoes evenly over the crust, place a leaf of basil on top of each tomato, and sprinkle the Asiago cheese evenly over the tomatoes.

Bake the pizza on the bottom rack of a 500°F preheated oven for 8–10 minutes or until the crust is golden brown. Let the pizza cool for 20 minutes before serving.

Pizza Trivia

In Naples in the late 1800s street vendors known as the *lazzari* walked the city's streets selling pizza by the slice. A piece was purchased, folded in half lengthwise, and eaten on the run. The folded slices were called *libretti* or "little books." Years later in New York City, slices of pizza took on the name *folder.* In high school when we wanted to grab a slice of pizza, we would say "Let's go get a folder."

CHICKEN GUMBO PIZZA

Here is a pizza that captures the flavors of Louisiana to a fare-thee-well.

Makes one 14-inch pizza

> ¾ cup unbleached all-purpose flour
> 1 teaspoon salt
> 1 teaspoon garlic powder
> ½ teaspoon cayenne pepper
> 1 whole skinless, boneless chicken breast, cut into small cubes
> 2 tablespoons peanut or vegetable oil
> ¼ cup diced green bell pepper
> ¼ cup diced onion
> ½ cup frozen cut okra
> 1 cup low-salt chicken broth
> 2 tablespoons tomato paste
> Salt and feshly ground black pepper to taste
> 1 recipe Basic Pizza Dough II (page 25)
> 1 cup shredded smoked mozzarella

Combine ½ cup of the flour, salt, garlic powder, and cayenne pepper in a plastic resealable bag. Add the cubes of chicken and toss well to coat the chicken thoroughly.

In a sauté pan over medium-high heat, warm the oil for 1 minute. Add the chicken, shaking off any excess flour. Cook and stir until the chicken is cooked through, about 4 minutes. Set the chicken aside. Drain the pan, but don't wash it.

Add the green pepper, onion, and okra to a pan of boiling salted water and boil for 4 minutes. Drain thoroughly and reserve.

Set the same pan in which the chicken was cooked back over medium-high heat. Add the remaining flour and cook and stir for about 1 minute. Turn the heat to high and add the chicken broth. Scrape and stir the pan while reducing the liquid to about ½ cup. Stir in the tomato paste. Cook and stir for about 3 minutes or until a smooth, slightly thick paste or roux is formed. Add salt and pepper to taste. Reserve.

With your fingers, press and form a ½-inch border around the crust.

Spread the tomato roux evenly over the pizza crust up to the border. Add the reserved vegetables and the chicken, spreading them evenly over the crust. Sprinkle on the smoked mozzarella.

Bake the pizza on the bottom rack of a preheated 500°F oven for 8–10 minutes or until the crust is brown and the cheese is melted and starts to take on color.

Pizza Party

For your next pizza party, make two hearty pizzas, Chicken Vesuvio Pizza (page 92) and Pancetta and Potato Pizza (page 82), which both use potatoes and Pat's Favorite Pizza Dough recipe. Make one of each or, if you prefer, both the same by doubling the topping ingredients. If you need more than two pizzas, make two batches of dough.

CHICKEN VESUVIO PIZZA

Makes one 13- to 14-inch pizza

> 2 whole skinless, boneless chicken breasts
> Freshly ground black pepper to taste
> ¼ cup olive oil
> 2 large (about 1½ pounds) redskin potatoes, peeled and cut into small cubes
>   (about 2 cups)
> 2 teaspoons minced garlic
> 1 tablespoon chopped fresh oregano or 1 teaspoon dried, crumbled
> 1 tablespoon chopped fresh basil or 1 teaspoon dried, crumbled
> 1 tablespoon chopped fresh rosemary or 1 teaspoon dried, crumbled
> ½ teaspoon salt
> 1 shell from Pat's Favorite Pizza Dough (page 23)
> ¼ cup freshly grated Parmesan cheese

Pat the chicken breasts dry. Sprinkle with pepper.

In a sauté pan over medium-high heat, warm 2 tablespoons of the oil for 1 minute. Add the chicken breasts (in two batches if necessary, adding more oil as needed) and sauté for 3 minutes on each side or until cooked through. Cut the chicken into ¼-inch cubes. Set aside.

Cook the potatoes in boiling salted water for 5 minutes or until barely tender. Drain and reserve.

In a large bowl, toss the chicken with the potatoes and the remaining 2 tablespoons of oil. Add the garlic, herbs, salt, and ½ teaspoon pepper and toss to combine.

With your fingers, press and form a 1-inch border around the crust.

Spread the chicken and potato mixture over the crust and sprinkle on the grated Parmesan cheese.

Bake the pizza on the bottom rack of a preheated 500°F oven for 8–10 minutes or until the crust is brown and crispy.

RICKY'S RICOTTA PIZZA

Ricotta adds a certain creaminess to this pizza, which by any other name would simply be a pizza with Italian sausage. This is not like any sausage pizza you've had before.

Makes one 12- to 13-inch pizza

> ⅓ pound sweet Italian sausage, casing removed
> 1 recipe Basic Pizza Dough II (page 25)
> ½ cup all-purpose ground tomatoes
> ½ cup ricotta cheese
> ¼ pound mozzarella cheese, shredded (about 1 cup)
> ½ teaspoon dried oregano, crumbled

In a small skillet over medium heat, cook the sausage, breaking up the larger chunks with the edge of a wooden spoon, until there is no trace of red left. Set aside.

With your fingers, press and form a ½-inch border around the crust.

Spread the tomatoes evenly over the crust (the coverage will be minimal, but that's what we are after).

Drop the ricotta in 1-tablespoon dollops (about seven in all) over the tomatoes, spacing them as evenly as possible. Arrange the sausage evenly over the pizza. Sprinkle on the mozzarella cheese, then the oregano.

Bake the pizza on the bottom rack of a preheated 500°F oven for 10–12 minutes, until the crust is golden brown and the cheese is beginning to take on brown speckles.

Pizza Trivia

There are more than
58,000 pizzerias in the United States.

PATSY'S FAMOUS FUNGHI PIZZA

My father was a commercial mushroom farmer for a number of years, and in my teens I spent a lot of time picking mushrooms. This pizza is dedicated to him. No tomatoes are used here; nothing stands in the way of the woodsy and earthy flavor of the mushrooms.

Makes one 14-inch pizza

3 tablespoons extra-virgin olive oil

2 cloves garlic, minced

½ pound shiitake mushrooms, sliced

½ pound portobello mushrooms, sliced about ¼ inch thick

½ pound cultivated mushrooms, sliced about ⅛ inch thick

2 teaspoons dried oregano, crumbled

Salt and freshly ground black pepper to taste

1 recipe Basic Pizza Dough II (page 25)

½ pound mozzarella cheese, shredded (about 2 cups)

In a large sauté pan or skillet over medium-high heat, warm the olive oil for 1 minute. Add the garlic and the mushrooms and cook and stir until the mushrooms start to give off their liquid and the portobello slices are still fairly firm, about 4 minutes. Add the oregano and combine. Add salt and pepper to taste. Turn the mushrooms out of the pan onto a large plate and reserve.

With your fingers, press and form a ½-inch border around the crust.

Spread the mushroom mixture evenly over the crust. Sprinkle on the cheese.

Bake the pizza on the bottom rack of a preheated 500°F oven for 10 minutes or until the crust is brown and the cheese melts and starts to take on color.

EGGPLANT PARMIGIANA PIZZA

Look for eggplant that is firm when pressed and as slim and tapered as possible; it's fresher and generally has fewer seeds. Fewer seeds means less bitterness, which means that the eggplant doesn't have to be salted and pressed to rid it of its bitter juice.

On more than one occasion I have enjoyed this pizza after it has been sitting at room temperature for several hours, so it doesn't need to be served directly from the oven.

Makes one 12- by 15-inch pizza

> 1 recipe Basic Pizza Dough II (page 25)
> 1 eggplant (about 1 pound), washed and sliced into rounds about ⅛ inch thick
> 1 cup tomato puree or all-purpose ground tomatoes
> 2 cloves garlic, crushed
> 1 tablespoon chopped fresh oregano or 1 teaspoon dried, crumbled
> 1 tablespoon chopped fresh basil or 1 teaspoon dried, crumbled
> ⅛ teaspoon freshly ground black pepper
> Salt to taste
> 2 tablespoons olive oil
> 2 tablespoons freshly grated Parmesan cheese
> ½ pound mozzarella, shredded (about 2 cups)

After the dough has doubled in bulk, do not punch it down; set it in the middle of a lightly oiled 12- by 15-inch pan such as a jelly-roll pan. With your palm and fingers, press and stretch the dough to fit the pan, pushing it snugly up against the sides. The dough may tend to shrink back at first, so let it rest for 5 minutes or so, and it will stretch easier. Set aside.

Place the slices of eggplant on a baking sheet and brush lightly with olive oil. Place the pan under a preheated broiler and broil for 3–4 minutes on each side or until the eggplant just starts to take on color. You may need to do this in two batches. Set aside.

In a small mixing bowl, combine the tomatoes, garlic, oregano, basil, pepper, and salt to taste. Spread the tomatoes evenly over the pizza crust, leaving a ½-inch border all around. Arrange the eggplant slices over the tomatoes. Drizzle the olive oil over the eggplant. Sprinkle on the Parmesan, followed by the mozzarella.

Bake the pizza on the bottom rack of a preheated 450°F oven for 12–15 minutes, until the crust is golden brown and the cheese is bubbly and begins to take on color.

STUFFED SPINACH PIZZA

A classic pizza that got its start in Chicago but now is available around the country. Stuffed pizza is really an adaptation of a pizza known as *sfinciuni*, a pizza well known to the citizens of Palermo, Sicily. The main difference is the absence of sauce on the *sfinciuni*.

Makes one 9-inch stuffed pizza

> 1 recipe Basic Pizza Dough II (page 25)
> 4 cups tightly packed fresh spinach with no thick stems (about ½ pound), washed,
>   dried, and chopped coarse
> ½ pound mozzarella cheese, shredded (about 2 cups)
> ¼ cup freshly grated Parmesan cheese
> 1 28-ounce can Italian-style plum tomatoes, drained, crushed in the can with your hand,
>   and drained again
> 2 teaspoons chopped fresh basil or ½ teaspoon dried, crumbled
> 2 teaspoons chopped fresh oregano or ½ teaspoon dried, crumbled
> 1 clove garlic, pressed
> Salt and freshy ground black pepper to taste

Divide the dough into two equal pieces and roll each piece on a lightly floured surface to a thickness of ⅛ inch or less. Lay one piece of dough into a lightly oiled 9-inch pie pan or layer cake pan that is 1½ inches deep. The dough should fall over the sides of the pan by at least 1 inch.

In a mixing bowl, combine the spinach, mozzarella, and Parmesan cheeses. Put the mixture into the pan and lay the second piece of dough on top. Press down on the dough and filling with your hand to level the top. Press the two pieces of dough against the side of the pan to seal all around to form a shallow well. Trim off the excess dough. Roll and seal the edge of the two pieces of dough all around. Cut a slit in the middle of the dough with a sharp knife to allow the steam to escape. Set aside.

In a mixing bowl, combine the drained tomatoes, basil, oregano, and garlic. Add salt and pepper to taste. Crush and mix the tomato mixture with the back of a wooden spoon. Spoon the tomatoes evenly over the crust.

Bake the pizza on the bottom rack of a preheated 475°F oven for 20 minutes or until the crust is golden brown and starts to pull away from the sides of the pan. Let the pizza rest for 5 minutes before cutting and serving.

DEEP-DISH PIZZA FOR ONE

A scaled-down version of Chicago's famous pizza. Just the right amount for one hungry person.

Makes one 9-inch deep-dish pizza

> *1 ball of Beer Crust dough (page 27)*
> *6 ⅛-inch-thick slices (about ¼ pound) mozzarella cheese*
> *¾ cup drained, crushed Italian-style plum tomatoes*
> *½ teaspoon chopped fresh oregano or ⅛ teaspoon dried, crumbled*
> *½ teaspoon chopped fresh basil or ⅛ teaspoon dried, crumbled*
> *1 garlic clove, pressed*
> *1 tablespoon freshly grated Parmesan cheese*

Press the dough into a lightly oiled 9-inch layer cake or pie pan that is 1½ inches deep and pull the dough up the sides of the pan, pressing it with your fingers to a thickness of about ⅛ inch.

Lay the cheese slices evenly over the dough, overlapping them slightly.

In a small mixing bowl, combine the tomatoes, oregano, basil, and garlic and combine well.

Spread the tomato sauce evenly over the cheese. Sprinkle on the Parmesan cheese.

Bake the pizza on the bottom rack of a preheated 475°F oven for 18–20 minutes or until the crust is brown and pulls away from the sides of the pan. Let the pizza sit for about 10 minutes before cutting.

OPTIONS
In the topping, try cooked and crumbled Italian sausage, pepperoni, onion, or bell pepper.

CHICAGO DEEP-DISH PIZZA

This is the pizza that put Chicago on the pizza map. Usually the dough is made with more oil and the addition—in some cases—of a food coloring called *egg shade,* which gives the crust a yellow cast (some people think that it's cornmeal added to the dough recipe). I chose to cut back on the oil a bit and to omit the egg shade (it's hard to find anyway). Still, this is a pizza that is loaded with flavor.

To bring this dough to perfection, make the dough the night before you plan to serve the pizza. Matters proceed in a slightly different fashion with a classic deep-dish pizza—the cheese goes on top of the dough, not over the tomatoes. Other than that, the only thing to watch for is that the tomatoes are not carrying excess water.

This big 14-inch pizza can easily feed four people.

Makes one 14-inch deep-dish pizza

DOUGH

1 cup warm water (105–115°F)
1 ¼-ounce envelope (2½ teaspoons) active dry yeast
2 teaspoons sugar
3 cups unbleached all-purpose flour
2 teaspoons salt
¼ cup corn oil
2 teaspoons olive oil

Pour the water into a large mixing bowl or the bowl of a stand mixer. Sprinkle the yeast over the water. Add the sugar and stir to dissolve. Let stand for 10 minutes.

Add the flour and salt to the water and stir to combine. Add the corn oil and mix until a dough is formed. Knead the dough for a full 6–7 minutes or until it is completely smooth and satiny. (The dough can also be made in the food processor, in which case use cool water.)

Lightly dust a large bowl with flour. Place the dough ball into the bowl, dust the top with flour, and cover with plastic wrap and aluminum foil. Let sit on the kitchen counter for 20 minutes. Place the dough in the refrigerator overnight.

The next day, take the dough out of the refrigerator. *Don't punch down the dough.* Lightly oil a 14-inch pizza pan that is 2 inches deep using the olive oil. Remove the dough from the bowl by slipping your hand underneath it and place it in the center of the pan. Using your palms, stretch and push the dough toward the edge of the pan (as the dough warms up it will be easier to stretch). Pull the dough up the sides of the pan, pressing it against the sides with your fingers (only about ¼ inch of the pan sides should be showing) until it is quite thin. Cover and set aside. (The dough can be prepared to this point and held, covered, for about 1 hour or until the toppings are prepared.)

TOPPING

1 pound sweet Italian sausage, casing removed

2 28-ounce cans Italian-style plum tomatoes, drained

2 cloves garlic, pressed

1 teaspoon dried oregano, crumbled

1 teaspoon dried basil, crumbled

Salt and freshly ground black pepper to taste

¾ pound mozzarella cheese, sliced ⅛ inch thick

3 tablespoons freshly grated Parmesan cheese

In a sauté pan over medium heat, cook the sausage, breaking it up and pushing down on it with the back of a wooden spoon to form large, thick chunks, until it is just cooked through, about 4 minutes. Drain excess grease from the pan. Set aside.

Put the tomatoes in a mixing bowl. Crush completely with your hands and drain. Crush some more and drain again. You should have about 2 cups. Add the garlic, oregano, basil, and salt and pepper to taste and combine. Set aside.

Arrange the cheese slices, overlapping them slightly, over the crust. Spread the tomato mixture evenly over the cheese. Sprinkle on the Parmesan cheese and arrange the sausage evenly over the tomatoes.

Bake the pizza on the bottom rack of a preheated 450°F oven for 18–20 minutes or until the crust is golden and pulls away from the sides of the pan. Let the pizza sit for 10 minutes before serving.

OPTIONS

In the topping, try pepperoni slices, bell pepper, onion, or mushrooms, alone or in combination, at your discretion.

PEPPERONI RING PIZZA

A pizza with a hole in the middle. No, it's not a gimmick. This is a great pizza for an appetizer table or buffet because the crust on both sides of the slice makes it an easy-to-handle finger food. You can use the dough cut from the center to make an individual-size pizza.

Makes one 14-inch pizza

> 1 recipe Basic Pizza Dough II (page 25)
> ¾ cup Herbed Tomato Sauce (page 37) or tomato puree seasoned with
>   ½ teaspoon each of dried oregano and dried basil, crumbled
> ½ cup shredded mozzarella cheese
> 15–16 slices pepperoni

On a lightly floured surface, roll the ball of dough into a circle about 13 inches in diameter. Transfer the dough to a flat pizza pan.

Lay a round plate or saucer about 5 inches in diameter in the center of the dough. Cut around the edge of the plate with a knife. Remove the center piece of dough. With your fingers, press and form a ½-inch border around the outside and inside edges of the dough.

Spread the sauce evenly around the ring. Sprinkle the mozzarella evenly over the sauce. Arrange the slices of pepperoni over the cheese, evenly around the ring.

Bake the pizza on the bottom rack of a preheated 500°F oven for 8–10 minutes or until the crust is golden brown.

SPINACH PIZZA PIE

One of my favorite side dishes is spinach sautéed with garlic and olive oil. Here that idea, plus provolone and Parmesan cheese, becomes a spinach pizza pie.

Makes one 12-inch pizza

> 1 large ball of Whole-Wheat Pizza Dough (page 30)
> ¼ cup water
> 1 10-ounce package fresh spinach, washed thoroughly and thick stems removed
> 3 tablespoons extra-virgin olive oil
> 2 cloves garlic, minced
> ⅛ teaspoon freshly ground black pepper
> ⅛ teaspoon salt
> ¼ cup chopped scallions, white part only
> ¼ cup freshly grated Parmesan cheese
> ¾ cup (about ¼ pound) shredded provolone cheese

On a lightly floured surface, roll the dough into a circle 12 inches in diameter. With your fingers, press and form a ½-inch border around the crust. Cover with plastic wrap or a kitchen towel until you're ready to use it.

Put the water in a saucepan or deep sauté pan set over low heat. Add the spinach and cook, covered, until the leaves begin to wilt, about 4 minutes. Uncover and drain all excess water from the pan.

Add to the spinach the olive oil and garlic. Cook and stir over medium-high heat until the spinach is heated through, about 3 minutes. (The recipe can be made up to this point and held at room temperature for 3–4 hours.) Add the pepper and salt. Remove the spinach from the pan and let it cool slightly.

Spread the spinach mixture over the reserved crust up to the border. Sprinkle the scallions over the spinach. Sprinkle on the Parmesan and provolone.

Bake the pizza on the bottom rack of a preheated 500°F oven for 10–12 minutes or until the crust is golden brown and the cheese just begins to take on color.

PIZZA WITH TURKEY MARINARA

Using ground turkey gives this pizza a deliciously meaty flavor but without all the fat. Adding fennel seeds to the turkey makes the illusion that it is Italian sausage complete. Milk makes the dough soft inside, crispy outside.

Makes two 12- to 13-inch pizzas

DOUGH

2 level tablespoons (1 ounce) fresh yeast
¾ cup warm water (105–115°F)
3 cups unbleached all-purpose flour
1 teaspoon salt
¼ cup milk

In a measuring cup or bowl, dissolve the yeast in ½ cup of the warm water and allow to sit for 5 minutes.

In a large mixing bowl or the bowl of a stand mixer, combine the flour and salt.

Add the yeast mixture to the flour. Add the milk and the remaining water. With your hands, combine the dough into a ball. Turn the dough out of the bowl and knead for 5 minutes, until smooth. The dough should feel slightly damp.

Put the dough in a lightly oiled 4-quart bowl. Cover the bowl with plastic wrap and a kitchen towel and let rise for 1½–2 hours, until doubled in bulk.

Divide the dough into two pieces. On a lightly floured surface, roll each piece of dough into a circle 12–13 inches in diameter. Transfer one pizza crust to a pizza pan. Cover the second pizza crust with plastic wrap until you're ready to use it.

TOPPING

¾ pound ground turkey

2 teaspoons fennel seed

1 16-ounce can tomato puree or *1 recipe Fragrant Tomato Sauce (page 36)*

1 tablespoon chopped fresh oregano or *1 teaspoon dried, crumbled*

1 tablespoon chopped fresh basil or *1 teaspoon dried, crumbled*

Salt to taste

¾ pound mozzarella cheese, shredded (about 3 cups)

In a large skillet over medium-high heat, sauté the turkey with the fennel seed until the turkey is cooked through, about 5 minutes. Drain off any excess liquid.

In a mixing bowl, combine the tomato puree with the oregano and basil. Add salt to taste and stir to combine (if using the Fragrant Tomato Sauce, omit the oregano and basil).

Spread half of the tomato puree over each pizza crust to within ½ inch of the edge. Spread half of the ground turkey over the tomatoes on each. Spread half of the cheese over the turkey on each pizza.

Bake the pizza on the bottom rack of a preheated 500°F oven for 10–12 minutes or until the crust is brown and slightly crispy.

Pizza Trivia

Each year, thousands of people involved in the pizza industry attend Pizza Expo, the world's largest pizza-only trade show, held in Las Vegas in either February or March.

PIZZA WITH SPINACH AND PANCETTA

You will note that in this pizza recipe I use the half-and-half cheese method—half the cheese directly on the crust, the toppings, then the remaining cheese. This method gives the pizza a lot more eye appeal since the toppings are visible.

Makes one 12-inch pizza

> 1 10-ounce package fresh spinach
> ½ cup water
> 2 cloves garlic, pressed
> 1 tablespoon olive oil
> Freshly ground black pepper to taste
> ¼ pound pancetta, chopped (about ¾ cup)
> ¼ cup pine nuts
> 1 large ball of Whole-Wheat Pizza Dough (page 30)
> ½ pound smoked mozzarella, shredded (about 2 cups)

Wash and drain the spinach, but do not dry it. Place the water in a large pot, add the spinach, and over medium-high heat cook the spinach, covered, for 8–10 minutes or until it is wilted and soft. Drain the water from the pot. Return the pan to the heat and cook and stir until most of the water has evaporated. Add the garlic and olive oil and stir to combine. Stir in the pepper. Cook the spinach mixture, stirring, for 2 minutes longer. Transfer the spinach to a small mixing bowl.

In a small nonstick skillet, cook the pancetta over medium-high heat, stirring, for 8 minutes or until it starts to crisp slightly. Add the pancetta to the spinach.

In the same skillet in which the pancetta was cooked, toast the pine nuts over medium heat, stirring, until they turn a light brown, about 5 minutes. Watch the heat; pine nuts burn easily. Put the pine nuts on a plate or in a bowl.

Press or roll out the dough into a circle about 12 inches in diameter and place it on a lightly oiled flat pizza pan or a lightly floured pizza peel. With your fingers, press and form a ½-inch border around the crust.

Spread half of the smoked mozzarella evenly over the crust. Spread the spinach mixture evenly over the cheese. Sprinkle on the remaining cheese. Sprinkle the pine nuts evenly over the top layer of cheese, pressing them into the cheese with your fingers.

Bake the pizza on the bottom rack of a preheated 500°F oven for 8–10 minutes or until the crust is golden brown.

Pizza Party

Have a pizza party with Pizza with Spinach and Pancetta (page 104) and Pizza with Fresh Fennel and Sausage (page 106). It brings together two completely different flavor ideas while keeping a common taste thread—pork. In Pizza with Spinach and Pancetta it is the pancetta that stands out. In the other pizza fresh fennel and Italian sausage, a distinguished combination, share the taste stage. Both recipes use Whole-Wheat Pizza Dough.

PIZZA WITH FRESH FENNEL AND SAUSAGE

The half-and-half cheese method—half of the cheese under the toppings and half over—lets the toppings peek through.

Makes one 12-inch pizza

> 1 bulb fresh fennel (about 1 pound)
> 1 tablespoon olive oil
> ½ pound sweet Italian sausage, casing removed
> 1 large ball of Whole-Wheat Pizza Dough (page 30)
> ½ pound mozzarella cheese, shredded (about 2 cups)
> 3 tablespoons freshly grated Parmesan cheese

Trim the top of the fennel down to the bulb end. Pull off the outer layer of the bulb. Cut the bulb in half lengthwise and cut away the hard triangular core. Cut each half of the bulb lengthwise into ½-inch slices.

Put the fennel into a pot of lightly salted boiling water and cook until barely tender, about 5 minutes. Drain and reserve.

Warm the oil in a skillet over medium-high heat for 1 minute. Add the sausage and cook and stir, breaking the sausage into ½-inch chunks with the edge of a wooden spoon, until the sausage is cooked through, about 4 minutes. Drain excess fat from the skillet and reserve.

Press or roll out the dough ball into a circle about 12 inches in diameter and place it on a lightly oiled flat pizza pan or a lightly floured pizza peel. With your fingers, press and form a ½-inch border around the crust.

Sprinkle half of the mozzarella evenly over the crust up to the border. Arrange the fennel over the cheese. Arrange the sausage over the fennel. Sprinkle on the remaining mozzarella cheese, then the Parmesan.

Bake the pizza on the bottom rack of a preheated 500°F oven for 8–10 minutes or until the crust is golden brown.

Chapter 9

PIZZA WITH AN INTERNATIONAL FLAIR

PIZZA BISTEC

Makes one 13- to 14-inch pizza

> *1 shell from Pat's Favorite Pizza Dough (page 23)*
> *½ pound boneless sirloin steak, trimmed of fat*
> *3 tablespoons olive oil*
> *¾ cup drained and rinsed canned black beans*
> *¼ cup chopped cilantro*
> *½ cup chopped green bell pepper*
> *2 small cloves garlic, minced*
> *½ cup chopped onion*
> *1 28-ounce can Italian-style plum tomatoes, drained, crushed in the can by hand, and drained again*
> *1 teaspoon dried oregano, crumbled*
> *⅛ teaspoon freshly ground black pepper*
> *¼ cup chopped fresh green chilies**
> *½ pound smoked mozzarella, shredded (about 2 cups)*

Prick the pizza shell with the tines of a fork and bake it in a preheated 500°F oven for 4 minutes to set the crust. Set aside. Reduce the oven temperature to 450°F.

Cut the steak into ⅛-inch slices and then into ½-inch pieces. In a sauté pan over medium-high heat, warm 1 tablespoon of the oil for 1 minute. Add the steak and cook to medium-rare, stirring frequently, about 2 minutes. Set aside.

In a large mixing bowl, combine the beans, cilantro, bell pepper, garlic, onion, and remaining oil. Set aside.

In a separate bowl, combine the tomatoes, oregano, pepper, and chilies.

Spread the tomato mixture evenly over the parbaked pizza crust. Spread the bean mixture evenly over the tomatoes. Distribute the steak evenly over the bean mixture. Sprinkle the pizza with the cheese.

Bake the pizza on the bottom rack of a preheated 450°F oven for 10 minutes or until the crust is golden brown and the cheese melted.

---

* Do not touch your eyes when handling hot chilies and wash your hands well when finished.

PIZZA PATATAS CON RIOJANA

Patatas alla Riojana is an intensely flavored potato dish that is much favored by the winery owners of the Rioja region of northern Spain. None of the flavor is lost in this adaptation of the dish as a pizza topping.

Makes one 13- to 14-inch pizza

> *1 shell from Pat's Favorite Pizza Dough (page 23)*
> *¾ pound new potatoes, peeled and cut into small cubes (about 2 cups)*
> *2 tablespoons olive oil*
> *4 scallions, including 2 inches of green top, chopped*
> *½ cup chopped onion*
> *2 28-ounce cans Italian-style plum tomatoes, drained, crushed by hand in the can, and drained again*
> *1 large red bell pepper, roasted and peeled (page 48) and cut into strips*
> *¼ cup finely chopped cilantro*
> *½ teaspoon dried oregano, crumbled*
> *⅛ teaspoon ground cumin*
> *½ teaspoon salt*
> *⅛ teaspoon ground pepper*
> *½ pound Asiago or fontina cheese, shredded (about 2 cups)*

Prick the pizza shell with the tines of a fork and bake in a preheated 500°F oven for 4 minutes to set the crust. Set aside. Reduce the oven temperature to 450°F.

Cook the potatoes in boiling salted water until barely tender, about 8 minutes. Drain and set aside.

In a large sauté pan over medium heat, warm the olive oil for 1 minute. Add the scallions and onion and sauté, stirring, for 2 minutes. Add the tomatoes, bell pepper, cilantro, oregano, cumin, salt, and pepper. Turn the heat to high and cook the mixture, stirring occasionally, crushing the larger pieces of tomato, until it is reduced to 2 cups, about 10 minutes. Cool for 10 minutes before using.

Spread the tomato mixture evenly over the parbaked crust, leaving a ½-inch border. Arrange the cooked potatoes on top. Sprinkle on the cheese.

Bake the pizza on the bottom rack of a preheated 450°F oven for 10–12 minutes or until the crust is golden brown and the cheese has melted.

Pizza Party

Pizza Patatas con Riojana (page 110) and Pizza Bistec (page 109) can be combined for a pizza party with a Latin American flavor. Over the past few years I have been working on a pizza project in Mexico City and in the process have had a chance to sample a wide variety of Mexican food. Complex flavors are behind the pleasures of Mexican food, and these pizzas are loaded with flavor. If you parbake the crust and get all of the topping ingredients ready (each of these steps can be done several hours ahead and all but the crust refrigerated), the final assembly and baking take no time at all, so you can enjoy your pizza party to its fullest with your friends.

SHRIMP AND BLACK BEAN PIZZA

A version of a pizza that I encountered a few years ago in a seaside village in Mexico. It has surf-and-turf connotations—beans and shrimp—with just the right blend of herbs to pump up the flavor. Do not use precooked shrimp; you won't like the tough and overcooked taste.

Makes one 14-inch pizza

> 1 15-ounce can black beans, drained and rinsed
> ¼ cup chopped red onion
> ½ teaspoon ground cumin
> 1 teaspoon finely chopped chipotle peppers in adobo sauce★
> 1 clove garlic, minced
> ½ pound fresh plum tomatoes, diced (about 1 cup)
> ¼ cup chopped scallions
> 2 tablespoons olive oil
> 1 recipe Basic Pizza Dough II (page 25)
> 6 extra-large (16–20 per pound) fresh shrimp, shelled, cut in half lengthwise, and
>   rinsed under running cold water (this will get rid of the black vein)
> 3 tablespoons chopped cilantro

In a large bowl, combine the beans, onion, cumin, chipotle peppers, garlic, tomatoes, and scallions. Add the olive oil and toss to combine. Set aside.

With your fingers, press and form a ½-inch border around the crust.

Spread the bean mixture evenly over the crust up to the border. Arrange the shrimp evenly over the beans. Sprinkle on the cilantro.

Bake the pizza on the bottom rack of a preheated 500°F oven for 8–10 minutes or until the crust is golden brown.

OPTIONS
Though I am not a big fan of cheese with seafood, a sprinkling of shredded Asiago or fontina cheese is a possibility. Use about ¼ pound, shredded.

★ Do not touch your eyes when handling hot peppers and wash your hands well when finished.

PIZZA MEXICANA

Pizza takes a sharp turn and heads for the border in this rousing combination of Mexican flavors. By changing the heat quotient of the salsa, you can temper or tame the pizza to taste.

Makes one 14-inch pizza

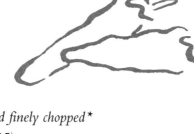

1 tablespoon vegetable oil
¾ pound ground turkey
1 teaspoon ground cumin
½ teaspoon salt
½ cup chopped onion
1 jalapeño pepper, stemmed, seeded, and finely chopped★
1 recipe Basic Pizza Dough II (page 25)
¾ cup bottled thick and chunky medium salsa
½ cup drained and rinsed canned black beans
1 cup shredded Monterey Jack cheese
1 cup shredded cheddar cheese
1 tablespoon finely chopped cilantro

In a sauté pan over medium heat, warm the oil for 1 minute. Add the ground turkey, cumin, salt, onion, and jalapeño. Cook and stir until the turkey is cooked through, 4 to 5 minutes, using a wooden spoon to break up the turkey. Pour off any excess fat from the pan.

With your fingers, press and form a ½-inch border around the crust.

Spread the salsa evenly over the crust up to the border. Sprinkle the black beans evenly over the salsa. Spread the reserved turkey evenly over the pizza. Combine the two cheeses and sprinkle evenly over the pizza. Sprinkle the cilantro evenly over the cheese.

Bake the pizza on the bottom rack of a preheated 500°F oven for 10 minutes or until the crust is brown and the cheese is melted and starting to take on color.

★ Do not touch your eyes when handling hot peppers and wash your hands well when finished.

CHICKEN AND BLACK BEAN PIZZA

A most flavorful pizza, one that brings into the pleasure picture the wonderful and exotic flavors of Mexican cooking. You can vary the heat by changing the amount and type of chilies used. For example, you can create a superhot version by using habanero or scotch bonnet chilies in place of milder green chilies.

Makes one 14-inch pizza

> *2 tablespoons vegetable or peanut oil*
>
> *¾ pound skinless, boneless chicken breast, sliced into ½-inch pieces*
>
> *Freshly ground black pepper to taste*
>
> *1 cup drained and rinsed canned black beans*
>
> *½ teaspoon ground cumin*
>
> *2 tablespoons fresh green chilies such as poblano or jalapeño, chopped**
>
> *1 pound fresh plum tomatoes, chopped*
>
> *2 cloves garlic, minced*
>
> *½ cup chopped cilantro*
>
> *1 recipe Basic Pizza Dough II (page 25)*
>
> *2 tablespoons olive oil*
>
> *½ pound Monterey Jack cheese, shredded (about 2 cups)*
>
> *1 teaspoon dried oregano, crumbled*

In a skillet over medium-high heat, warm the vegetable oil for 1 minute. Add the chicken and sauté, stirring frequently, until the chicken is just cooked through, about 3 minutes. Add pepper to taste. Transfer the chicken to a large mixing bowl and let cool for 10 minutes.

To the bowl with the chicken, add the beans, cumin, chilies, tomatoes, garlic, and cilantro and combine thoroughly.

With your fingers, press and form a ½-inch border around the crust.

* Do not touch your eyes when handling hot peppers and wash your hands well when finished.

Spread the chicken and tomato mixture evenly over the crust. Drizzle the olive oil evenly over the chicken mixture. Sprinkle on the cheese and oregano.

Bake the pizza on the bottom rack of a preheated 500°F oven for 10 minutes or until the crust is golden brown and the cheese has melted into the tomatoes.

OPTIONS

Replace the chicken with large shelled and deveined shrimp that have been butterflied and grilled or sautéed. You will need 8–10 large shrimp.

Pizza Trivia

Vincenzo Buonassisi, cookbook author and scholar, says this about eating pizza: "Let's be clear about this. You should always eat pizza with your hands, just as they do in Naples. It doesn't make sense to subject the pizza to the torture of a knife and fork while it cools, losing its flavor and aroma."

PIZZA ARREEBA!

A pizza with a good "burn"—the extra-spicy sauce takes care of that. It's easy to make too. Prepare the sauce and the turkey ahead, and then at the last moment assemble and bake. If you want a meatier flavor, replace the turkey with ground pork.

Makes one 14-inch pizza

> 1 tablespoon vegetable oil
> 1 pound ground turkey
> ⅛ teaspoon ground cumin
> 2 tablespoons minced cilantro
> ⅛ teaspoon freshly ground black pepper
> Salt to taste
> 1 recipe Basic Pizza Dough II (page 25)
> 1 cup Extra-Spicy Tomato Sauce (page 39)
> ¼ pound Monterey Jack cheese, shredded (about 1 cup)
> ¼ pound mild cheddar cheese, shredded (about 1 cup)
> Chopped cilantro for garnish (optional)

Add the vegetable oil to a sauté pan or skillet over medium-high heat. Add the ground turkey and cook and stir for 2 minutes. Add the cumin, cilantro, and pepper. Cook and stir for 2 minutes or until the turkey is just cooked through. Add salt to taste. Drain the excess liquid from the pan and set aside.

With your fingers, press and form a ½-inch border around the pizza crust.

Spread the sauce evenly over the pizza crust up to the border. Spread the turkey evenly over the sauce. In a small mixing bowl, combine the cheeses and sprinkle them evenly over the turkey.

Bake the pizza on the bottom rack of a preheated 500°F oven for 10 minutes or until the crust is golden brown. Sprinkle some chopped cilantro over the pizza just before serving if desired.

PIZZA FRIJOLES

Makes one 13-inch pizza

1 large ball of Unleavened Pizza Dough (page 29)
1 cup canned Spicy Ranchero refried beans
1 tablespoon water
¼ pound Monterey Jack cheese, shredded (about 1 cup)

On a lightly floured surface, roll the dough into a circle 13 inches in diameter. Transfer the dough to a flat pizza pan.

In a small bowl, stir together the refried beans and water. Spread the refried beans over the crust, leaving about a ½-inch border all around. Sprinkle the cheese evenly over the beans.

Bake the pizza on the bottom rack of a preheated 500°F oven for 8–10 minutes or until the edges bubble slightly and start to brown.

Pizza Party

Have a pizza party with Pizza Frijoles (above) and Pizza Frijoles Negros (page 118), two quick and easy pizzas that you can set in front of TV-watching sports fans in no time flat. Because the dough is unleavened, no rising time is involved, so from start to finish it's about a 30-minute trip, even faster if you use a food processor to make the dough.

PIZZA FRIJOLES NEGROS

Makes one 13-inch pizza

> *1 large ball of Unleavened Pizza Dough (page 29)*
> *⅔ cup bottled thick and chunky medium salsa*
> *1½ cups drained and rinsed canned black beans*
> *¼ pound Monterey Jack cheese, shredded (about 1 cup)*
> *¼ pound mild cheddar cheese, shredded (about 1 cup)*

On a lightly floured surface, roll the dough into a circle 13 inches in diameter. Transfer the dough to a flat pizza pan.

Spread the salsa over the crust, leaving about a ½-inch border all around. Spread the beans over the salsa. In a small bowl, combine the two cheeses. Sprinkle the cheese mixture evenly over the pizza.

Bake the pizza on the bottom rack of a preheated 500°F oven for 8–10 minutes or until the edges bubble slightly and start to brown.

Pizza Trivia

The world's largest pizza was built by Lorenzo Amato and Louis Piancone in Tallahassee, Florida. The pizza was 10,000 square feet and measured 140 feet across. It weighed in at 44,457 pounds.

LUIS'S SPECIAL

The popularity of salsa prompted the idea of adding salsa to the tomatoes for an extra kick. It works in a delicious way in this pizza, one that is deep with flavor and requires just a few toppings. There are many bottled salsas to choose from, so pick the one with the heat that you enjoy the most.

Makes one 14-inch pizza

> ¾ pound chorizo
> 1 28-ounce can Italian-style plum tomatoes
> ½ cup thick and chunky medium salsa
> 1 recipe Basic Pizza Dough II (page 25)
> 10 ounces Monterey Jack cheese, shredded (about 2½ cups)
> ¼ cup loosely packed chopped cilantro

In a sauté pan over medium-heat, crumble the chorizo and cook thoroughly while breaking up the larger pieces with a wooden spoon, about 4 minutes. Drain the grease from the pan. Transfer the chorizo to a dinner plate, smooth into one layer, and blot with paper towels to remove excess grease. Set aside.

Drain and crush the tomatoes until they measure 1 cup. Add the salsa to the tomatoes and blend thoroughly.

With your fingers, press and form a ½-inch border around the crust.

Arrange half the cheese evenly over the crust. Spoon the sauce evenly over the cheese in several globs. Sprinkle the remaining cheese over the sauce. Sprinkle the chorizo evenly over the cheese, pushing it into the cheese with your fingers or the back of a spoon. Sprinkle on the cilantro.

Bake the pizza on the bottom rack of a preheated 500°F oven for 10 minutes or until the crust is golden brown.

Chapter 10

VEGETARIAN PIZZA

PIZZA INSALATA

This salad pizza is a refreshing way to have your salad and your pizza at the same time. While the pizza with cheese is baking, assemble the salad. Pizza insalata is good anytime of year but especially in the summer, when fresh tomatoes are at peak flavor. If the pizza is served as a first course, it will serve four people easily. As a salad entree it will serve two generously.

Makes one 14-inch pizza

6–7 cups mixed lettuces—red leaf, leaf, radicchio
¼ cup sliced red onion (optional)
4–5 fresh plum tomatoes, seeded and cubed
½ cup extra-virgin olive oil
1 teaspoon balsamic vinegar
1 teaspoon fresh lemon juice
Salt and freshly ground black pepper to taste
1 recipe Quick-Rising Dough (page 26)
6–8 thin slices provolone cheese (about 6 ounces)

In a large mixing bowl, combine the lettuces, onion, and tomatoes. Set aside. (The salad—without the dressing—can be made ahead and refrigerated for several hours.)

In a small bowl or measuring cup, combine the olive oil, vinegar, and lemon juice. Whisk well to combine. Season with salt and pepper.

With your fingers, press and form a ½-inch border around the crust. Prick the base of the crust all over with a fork.

Lay the slices of cheese evenly over the crust up to the border.

Bake the pizza on the bottom rack of a preheated 450°F oven for 12–15 minutes, until the crust is golden brown and the cheese starts to take on brown speckles. Remove the pizza from the oven and allow to cool for about 10 minutes.

Toss the salad with the dressing. Cut the pizza into wedges and space them on a large serving plate. Arrange portions of the salad between the wedges and serve.

VERY TOMATO AND EGGPLANT PIZZA

Makes one 12-inch pizza

> *1 small, firm eggplant (about ½ pound)*
>
> *3 tablespoons Garlic-Infused Olive Oil (page 47)*
>
> *1 large ball of Whole-Wheat Pizza Dough (page 30)*
>
> *½ cup oil-packed sun-dried tomatoes (page 48), chopped*
>
> *12 leaves fresh basil*
>
> *7–8 (about 1 pound) fresh plum tomatoes, sliced into ¼-inch rounds*
>
> *1 tablespoon chopped fresh oregano or 1 teaspoon dried, crumbled*
>
> *¼ cup pine nuts, lightly toasted (see note)*

Trim the eggplant and slice it into rounds about ¼ inch thick. Arrange the eggplant in a single layer on a baking sheet and brush liberally with the Garlic-Infused Olive Oil. Broil the eggplant in batches on one side only in a preheated broiler about 4 inches from the heat until it begins to take on a deep brown color, about 4 minutes. Remove from the oven and set aside.

On a lightly floured surface, press or roll the dough into a circle 12 inches in diameter. With your fingers, press and form a ½-inch border around the crust.

Arrange the eggplant slices over the crust, overlapping them slightly if necessary. Sprinkle on the sun-dried tomatoes. Tear the basil leaves and sprinkle them over the pizza. Arrange the sliced plum tomatoes over the pizza and sprinkle on the oregano. Sprinkle the pine nuts evenly over the pizza.

Bake the pizza on the bottom rack of a preheated 500°F oven for 8–10 minutes or until the crust starts to turn dark brown.

Note: There are two easy methods for toasting pine nuts: (1) Put a teaspoon of olive oil in a small nonstick skillet and toast the pine nuts over medium heat, shaking the pan to toast them evenly and to prevent them from burning, or (2) strew the pine nuts over a small baking sheet or oven-proof pan and toast them in a preheated 350°F oven.

VERY VEGGIE PIZZA

Makes one 12-inch pizza

> *2 tablespoons olive oil*
> *½ cup chopped green bell pepper*
> *½ cup chopped red bell pepper*
> *¼ cup chopped red onion*
> *1 clove garlic, minced*
> *1 large ball of Whole-Wheat Pizza Dough (page 30)*
> *1 cup cooked broccoli florets*
> *1 cup chopped fresh tomato*
> *1 tablespoon chopped fresh oregano or 1 teaspoon dried, crumbled*
> *2 tablespoons Basil Olive Oil (page 45) or Garlic-Infused Olive Oil (page 47)*

In a sauté pan or skillet over medium-high heat, warm the oil for 1 minute. Add the peppers and onion and sauté, stirring occasionally, for 4 minutes. Add the garlic and cook for 1 minute. Transfer the mixture to a small mixing bowl and allow to cool while you roll out the dough.

On a lightly floured surface, press or roll the dough into a circle 12 inches in diameter.

Spread the pepper and onion mixture evenly over the crust up to the border. Arrange the broccoli florets evenly over the pizza, pushing them gently into the peppers. Sprinkle the tomato evenly over the pizza. Sprinkle on the oregano.

Bake the pizza on the bottom rack of a preheated 500°F oven for 8–10 minutes or until the crust starts to turn dark brown.

Remove the pizza from the oven and drizzle the olive oil evenly over it.

PIZZA WITH ESCAROLE AND PINE NUTS

I love the flavor of escarole sautéed with garlic and olive oil. With that as a base on which to build a tasty pizza, toasted pine nuts and smoked mozzarella are just so much icing. Note the order in which this pizza is built: cheese, escarole, cheese. The cheese base helps to prevent a soggy crust.

Makes one 14-inch pizza

¼ cup pine nuts

¼ cup water

1½ pounds escarole, trimmed and washed

2 tablespoons extra-virgin olive oil

2 cloves garlic, minced

⅛ teaspoon hot red pepper flakes

Salt and freshy ground black pepper to taste

1 recipe Basic Pizza Dough II (page 25)

¾ pound smoked mozzarella, shredded (about 3 cups)

In a small nonstick skillet over medium heat, cook and stir the pine nuts until golden brown, about 5 minues. Set aside.

Put the water and escarole in a large sauté pan or pot and cook, covered, over medium heat until the leaves have wilted and softened, 6–7 minutes. Drain any excess water from the pan.

Add the olive oil, garlic, and red pepper flakes to the pan. Cook and stir over medium heat for 4 minutes. Add salt and pepper to taste. Set aside and cool for 10 minutes. (The recipe can be made up to this point and held for several hours.)

With your fingers, press and form a ½-inch border around the crust.

Sprinkle half the cheese evenly over the pizza crust. Spread the escarole mixture evenly over the cheese. Sprinkle the remaining cheese evenly over the escarole. Sprinkle the pine nuts evenly over the pizza, pushing them gently into the cheese.

Bake the pizza on the bottom rack of a preheated 500°F oven for 10 minutes or until the crust is golden brown.

BEANS AND GREENS PIZZA

When I was a teenager, my mother occasionally made a dish with some fresh spinach or escarole, white beans, garlic, and cubes of day-old Italian bread. My brothers and I dubbed the dish "concrete" because of its appearance. There was no doubt, however, about the flavor, because we scraped our plates. With a bit of modification I've turned a hearty and simple dish into a great-tasting pizza. If you prefer, escarole can be used in place of the spinach.

Makes one 14-inch pizza

> 1 pound fresh spinach, washed and thicker stems removed
> ¼ cup water
> ¼ cup olive oil
> 2 cloves garlic, pressed
> ¼ cup chopped onion
> ⅛ teaspoon freshy ground black pepper
> ⅛ teaspoon salt
> ⅛ teaspoon hot red pepper flakes
> 1 19-ounce can cannellini, drained and rinsed
> 1 recipe Basic Pizza Dough II (page 25)
> ¾ pound mozzarella cheese, shredded (about 3 cups)

In a large sauté pan or saucepan over medium heat, wilt the spinach with the water, covered, for 3–4 minutes. Drain excess water from the pan and put the pan back on the heat, uncovered, for 2 minutes to evaporate any remaining water.

Add 3 tablespoons of the olive oil, the garlic, and the onion to the spinach. Cook and stir for 2 minutes. Add the pepper, salt, red pepper flakes, and beans and cook over medium heat, stirring to combine, for 2 minutes. Set aside to cool slightly for 10 minutes.

With your fingers, press and form a ½-inch border around the crust. Brush or rub the surface of the crust with the remaining olive oil.

Spread half the mozzarella evenly over the crust up to the border. Arrange the spinach and beans mixture evenly over the cheese. Sprinkle the remaining cheese on top.

Bake the pizza on the bottom rack of a preheated 500°F oven for 10–12 minutes or until the crust is golden brown and the cheese is speckled brown.

PIZZA WITH EGGPLANT AND TOMATOES

The flavor marriage of eggplant and fresh tomatoes is pure eating bliss. Buy eggplants that are small, firm, and have a tight skin, because they will have fewer seeds in the middle. Too many seeds give an eggplant bitterness, which can be removed only by salting and pressing.

Makes one 14-inch pizza

> *1–2 small, firm eggplants (about ¾ pound total)*
>
> *3–4 tablespoons (to taste) Garlic-Infused Olive Oil (page 47)*
>
> *1 recipe Basic Pizza Dough II (page 25)*
>
> *½ pound mozzarella cheese, shredded (about 2 cups)*
>
> *6–7 (about ¾ pound) fresh plum tomatoes, sliced crosswise ¼ inch thick*
>
> *1 tablespoon chopped fresh oregano or 1 teaspoon dried, crumbled*

Trim the stem end of the eggplant and slice lengthwise into ¼-inch slices. Arrange the eggplant on a broiler pan or baking sheet and brush each slice liberally with the oil. Broil the eggplant (in two batches if necessary) in a preheated broiler about 4 inches from the heat on one side only for 3–4 minutes or until the eggplant turns a russet brown. Remove the eggplant from the oven and set aside.

With your fingers, press and form a ½-inch border around the crust.

Sprinkle half the cheese evenly over the crust. Arrange the tomatoes evenly over the cheese and sprinkle on the oregano. Arrange the eggplant on the pizza in a flower or spoke pattern. Sprinkle the remaining cheese evenly over the eggplant.

Bake the pizza on the bottom rack of a preheated 500°F oven for 8–10 minutes or until the crust is golden brown.

FOUR-CHEESE VEGGIE PIZZA

If you love vegetables and you love cheese, you will fall head over heels in love with this pizza. There are two layers of cheese—the first layer directly on the crust, the second over the vegetables. No tomatoes are used. If you can't get frozen artichoke hearts, use artichoke hearts bottled in water, drained.

Makes two 13- to 14-inch pizzas

> 2 cloves garlic, pressed
> ½ cup olive oil
> ½ pound mozzarella cheese, shredded (about 2 cups)
> ½ pound provolone cheese, shredded (about 2 cups)
> ½ cup freshly grated Parmesan cheese
> ½ cup (about 2 ounces) shredded fontina cheese
> 1 recipe Pat's Favorite Pizza Dough (page 23)
> 1 9-ounce package frozen artichoke hearts, cooked according to package directions
>   and sliced thin
> 1½ cups thinly sliced zucchini (about 2 zucchini)
> 2 cups thinly sliced shiitake mushrooms
> 1 tablespoon fresh chopped oregano or 2 teaspoons dried, crumbled
> 1 tablespoon fresh chopped thyme or 1 teaspoon dried, crumbled

At least 1 hour before using, combine the garlic and olive oil in a small measuring cup.

In a mixing bowl, combine the four cheeses.

With your fingers, press and form a ½-inch border around each crust.

Brush each crust, including the border, with the garlic oil (save any extra, refrigerated, for another time).

Divide half of the cheese mixture between the two pizzas, spreading it evenly up to the border. Divide the vegetables evenly between the two pizzas. Sprinkle on the oregano. Divide the remaining cheese between the pizzas, spreading it evenly over the vegetables.

Bake the pizzas on the bottom rack of a preheated 500°F oven for 10–12 minutes or until the crust is golden brown and the cheese is melted and speckled brown.

ROASTED PEPPER AND TOMATO PIZZA

Makes one 12-inch pizza

> 1 shell from Beer Crust dough (page 27)
> ½ pound fontina or Asiago cheese, shredded (about 2 cups)
> 6 (¾–1 pound) large fresh plum tomatoes, sliced crosswise ¼ inch thick
> 2 tablespoons freshly grated Parmesan cheese
> 1 large red bell pepper, roasted and peeled (page 48) and cut into ½-inch strips
>   (about 16 strips in all) or ⅔ cup bottled roasted peppers cut into strips
> 15 leaves fresh basil

With your fingers, press and form a ½-inch border around the crust.

Sprinkle half the fontina evenly over the pizza crust. Arrange the tomatoes evenly over cheese. Sprinkle on the Parmesan. Arrange the bell pepper evenly over the pizza, then tear the basil leaves and sprinkle them on. Sprinkle on the remaining cheese.

Bake the pizza on the bottom rack of a preheated 500°F oven for 8–10 minutes or until the crust is golden brown.

Pizza Party

By making Pizza with Roasted Tomatoes and Ricotta (page 131) and Roasted Pepper and Tomato Pizza (above), you can throw a pizza party that takes full advantage of fresh vegetables and herbs when they are at their peak picking season: ripe plum tomatoes, fresh basil, and roasted fresh peppers are the tasty combinations.

PIZZA WITH ROASTED TOMATOES AND RICOTTA

Makes one 12-inch pizza

7–8 (about 1 pound) fresh plum tomatoes

1 cup ricotta cheese

⅛ teaspoon salt

⅛ teaspoon freshly ground black pepper

1 shell from Beer Crust dough (page 27)

1 tablespoon chopped fresh oregano or 1 teaspoon dried, crumbled

12–15 leaves fresh basil

2 tablespoons freshly grated Parmesan cheese

Cut about ¼ inch off the stem end of each tomato and cut the tomatoes in half crosswise. With your fingers or the end of a small spoon, scoop away the seeds. Lay the tomatoes, cut side down, on a baking sheet or broiler pan. Roast the tomatoes in a preheated broiler about 4 inches from the heat for 6 minutes or until the skin blisters and begins to turn black. Remove from the oven and pick off the loosened skin with the tines of a fork and discard. Squash the tomatoes gently with the back of a spoon. Allow the tomatoes to cool for 20 minutes.

In a small mixing bowl, combine the ricotta, salt, and pepper. Set aside.

With your fingers, press and form a ½-inch border around the crust.

Arrange the tomatoes evenly over the crust up to the border. Sprinkle on the oregano. Tear the basil and sprinkle it on. Using a large spoon, drop the ricotta in dollops, about 7 large dollops in all, evenly over the pizza. Sprinkle on the Parmesan.

Bake the pizza on the bottom rack of a preheated 500°F oven for 8–10 minutes or until the crust is golden brown.

Pizza Party

For people who are just plain staying away from dairy products, have a cheeseless pizza party, with Very Tomato and Eggplant Pizza (page 124) and Very Veggie Pizza (page 125). Use fresh herbs if at all possible—they definitely enhance the flavor.

Chapter 11

BREAKFAST AND BRUNCH PIZZA

BLANCA'S FAVORITE BRUNCH PIZZA

In an office adjoining my cooking school is a company—owned by a friend—that sells espresso machines and imported coffee. Blanca, who hails from Mexico City, works in that office as a tech specialist on espresso machines. A few years ago I made this pizza for Blanca and her friends, and it was an instant hit. Serve the pizza as part of a brunch buffet or for a hearty breakfast.

Makes one 14-inch pizza

> *¾ pound chorizo, crumbled*
> *1 recipe Basic Pizza Dough II (page 25)*
> *½ cup canned refried beans, thinned with 1 tablespoon warm water*
> *¾ cup bottled medium-hot salsa*
> *6 eggs, lightly beaten*
> *¼ cup chopped cilantro*
> *¼ pound cheddar cheese, shredded (about 1 cup)*
> *¼ pound Monterey Jack cheese, shredded (about 1 cup)*

In a sauté pan over medium heat, cook the chorizo, breaking up the larger pieces with a wooden spoon, about 5 minutes. Drain all the fat from the pan. Reserve.

With your fingers, press and form a ½-inch border around the crust.

Spread the refried beans over the crust up to the border. Spread the salsa over the beans.

In a nonstick skillet over medium-high heat, scramble the eggs just until they are set and no longer runny. Spread the eggs loosely over the salsa. Sprinkle the cilantro over the eggs. Combine the two cheeses and sprinkle evenly over the eggs. Sprinkle the reserved chorizo over the cheese, pushing it into the cheese with the back of a spoon.

Bake the pizza on the bottom rack of a preheated 450°F oven for 10–12 minutes or until the crust is golden brown and the cheese is melted and bubbly.

MAC'S BREAKFAST PIZZA

This is one great-tasting breakfast or brunch pizza. Make the dough the night before and put everything together in the A.M. in no time flat. The béchamel sauce can also be made the night before and refrigerated. It will get a bit tight, so loosen it up with milk or water to a thick yet spreadable consistency. One pizza should be enough for two people.

Makes one 10-inch pizza

BÉCHAMEL SAUCE

3 tablespoons unsalted butter
¼ cup unbleached all-purpose flour
¾ cup milk
⅛ teaspoon salt
Freshly ground black pepper to taste

THE REST

1 teaspoon unsalted butter
3 large eggs, lightly beaten
1 large ball of Whole-Wheat Pizza Dough (page 30)
4 3-inch-diameter slices Canadian bacon
¼ pound mild cheddar cheese, shredded (about 1 cup)

Make the béchamel sauce: In a small heavy saucepan, melt the butter over medium heat. Add the flour and cook and stir for 2 minutes. Off the heat, add the milk in a slow, steady stream while stirring. Over the heat, cook and stir the sauce until it smooths out and starts to thicken, about 3 minutes. Add the salt and pepper to taste. Set aside.

In a small nonstick skillet, melt the butter over medium heat until it just starts to foam. Stir in the eggs and scramble just until the eggs are set. Set aside.

Roll or press the dough into a 10-inch-diameter circle and place it on a flat pizza pan. With your fingers, press and form a ½-inch border around the crust.

Spread the béchamel sauce evenly over the crust up to the border. Arrange the Canadian bacon slices evenly over the pizza. Top the bacon slices with the eggs. Sprinkle the cheese over the pizza.

Bake the pizza on the bottom rack of a preheated 500°F oven for 8–10 minutes or until the crust is golden brown and the cheese is bubbly. Let rest for several minutes before cutting and serving.

OPTIONS

Use four strips of bacon, cooked crisp and crumbled, over the béchamel sauce instead of the Canadian bacon.

Pizza Trivia

Pepperoni is America's favorite pizza topping. Eel and squid are favorite toppings in Japan. Australians like shrimp and pineapple on their pizza, while Mexicans go for ham and pineapple, aka Hawaiian pizza.

PIZZA TORTILLA ESPAÑOLA

In the tapas bars in Spain one will always find a tortilla española or Spanish omelet. It is thick, always contains potatoes, and is served at room temperature. This pizza version is great for a brunch or buffet and can be served at room temperature. I have added chipotles in adobo sauce to zip up the flavor, but they can be omitted with no damage done. To get the extra strength needed in the crust, the dough is rolled a little thicker than usual.

Makes one 10-inch pizza

> *½ pound new potatoes, peeled and cut into small cubes (about 1 cup)*
> *¾ cup chopped bell pepper (green, red, or a combination)*
> *1 tablespoon extra-virgin olive oil*
> *¼ cup chopped onion*
> *1 teaspoon chopped canned chipotle peppers in adobo sauce**
> *4 extra-large eggs, lightly beaten*
> *⅛ teaspoon freshly ground black pepper*
> *Salt to taste*
> *1 large ball of Whole-Wheat Pizza Dough (page 30)*
> *6 ounces Manchego or white cheddar cheese, shredded (about 1½ cups)*
> *1 tablespoon chopped cilantro*

In a small saucepan, boil the cubed potatoes until barely tender, about 8 minutes. Drain and reserve.

In a small nonstick omelet pan or skillet over medium-high heat, sauté the bell pepper in the olive oil, stirring occasionally, for 3 minutes. Add the onion and cook for 3 minutes. Add the reserved potatoes and cook for 2 minutes. Add the chipotle peppers and stir to combine. (The dish can be made up to this point and held for 2 hours.)

Add the eggs and stir and cook until the eggs are no longer runny. Add the pepper and salt to taste. Transfer the mixture to a bowl or plate and allow to cool for 10 minutes.

---

* Use caution when working with the chipotle peppers. Remove them from the can with a fork, place them on a plate, and chop them with a knife and fork. If you have to touch the peppers with your hands, use rubber gloves. The smoky flavor of the chipotle is what makes this sauce. However, if canned chipotle peppers are not available, use fresh jalapeños.

Place the ball of dough on a lightly oiled flat pizza pan. With your hands, press the dough into a 10-inch circle. With your fingers, press and form a ¾-inch border around the crust.

Spread the egg and potato mixture evenly over the crust up to the border. Sprinkle on the cheese and spread it evenly over the pizza. Sprinkle the cilantro over the cheese.

Bake the pizza on the bottom rack of a preheated 500°F oven for 10 minutes or until the pizza crust is golden brown.

Pizza Trivia

As to which wines to drink with pizza, the answer is as simple as the wines themselves should be. As complex as the toppings might be on a New Wave pizza, there is still no need to go overboard. In fact, pizza was meant to be enjoyed with a young and inexpensive wine. And that means that on the white side it would be Soave, Orvieto, Chardonnay, Pinot Bianco, or Corvo. In the reds, a Bardolino, Valpolicella, Chianti, or Corvo would do just fine.

BEEF PICADILLO PIZZA

Picadillo implies some type of shredded meat or poultry. This recipe calls for beef, but ground pork or ground turkey will work just as well. A classic Mexican picadillo includes a number of sweet spices and raisins, both of which I chose to omit in favor of the more aromatic cilantro, thyme, and capers.

Makes one 14-inch pizza

> 1 tablespoon olive oil
> ½ cup chopped onion
> 1 cup chopped red bell pepper
> ½ pound ground round
> 15 green olives, pitted and chopped (about ½ cup)
> ⅛ teaspoon dried thyme, crumbled
> 2 tablespoons chopped cilantro
> 2 teaspoons drained capers
> ¾ cup tomato puree
> 1 recipe Basic Pizza Dough II (page 25)
> ½ pound Monterey Jack cheese, shredded (about 2 cups)

In a large sauté pan or skillet over medium-high heat, warm the oil for 1 minute. Add the onion, bell pepper, and ground round. Cook and stir until the meat is no longer red, about 3 minutes. Drain any excess grease from the pan.

Add the olives, thyme, cilantro, capers, and tomato puree to the pan. Stir and cook, simmering gently, for 3 minutes. (The sauce can be prepared and held for several hours or refrigerated overnight.)

With your fingers, press and form a ½-inch border around the crust.

Sprinkle half of the shredded cheese evenly over the crust. Spread the picadillo mixture evenly over the cheese up to the crust border. Sprinkle the remaining cheese over the pizza.

Bake the pizza on the bottom rack of a preheated 500°F oven for 8–10 minutes or until the crust is golden brown.

OPTIONS

For a spicier pizza, use a mixture of ½ cup tomato puree and ¼ cup bottled hot salsa. Alternatively, sliced fresh jalapeños can be added to the picadillo to taste.

PIZZA CASCINA

Cascina translates as farm. In other words, this is a farmer's breakfast pizza, one that starts the day off with a bang. It is not unusual for one person to eat an entire 8-inch pizza, so gauge the appetites of the eaters well and make and bake accordingly.

Makes two 8-inch pizzas

> *½ cup diced peeled redskin potatoes*
> *1 tablespoon olive oil*
> *½ cup diced bell pepper (green, red, or a combination)*
> *½ cup sweet Italian sausage meat*
> *4 eggs, lightly beaten*
> *⅛ teaspoon freshly ground black pepper*
> *1 large ball of Whole-Wheat Pizza Dough (page 30)*
> *¼ pound fontina cheese, shredded (about 1 cup)*

Cook the potatoes in boiling salted water until barely tender, about 8 minutes.

In a sauté pan over medium-high heat, warm the olive oil for 1 minute. Add the bell pepper and cook, covered, for 5 minutes or until just beginning to soften. Add the potatoes and sausage and cook, uncovered, until the sausage meat is cooked through, about 4 minutes. Drain any excess liquid from the pan.

Add the eggs to the skillet and stir and cook until the eggs just begin to set (do not cook the eggs firm). Add the pepper.

With your fingers, press and form a ½-inch border around the crust.

Divide the egg and potato mixture between the two pizza crusts. Top each pizza with half the grated cheese.

Bake the pizza on the bottom rack of a preheated 500°F oven for 8–10 minutes or until the crust is golden brown and the cheese is melted and bubbly.

PIZZA FRITTE

Throughout my youth a special treat on Saturday mornings were the small and puffy fried pizzas that my mother made. Piled on the plate alongside fried eggs and Italian sausage, they made a substantial breakfast that fueled my body for the day's work ahead. Fried pizza has many possibilities. It can be dipped in sugar, drizzled with honey, topped with a small amount of pizza sauce, sprinkled with grated Parmesan cheese . . . many delicious uses for pizza dough (and leftover pizza dough).

Use any of the dough recipes except the whole-wheat. Make sure the dough has had two rises since the warmer and more leavened the dough, the lighter the fried pizza will be.

Break off small pieces of dough and, with your fingers, press and pull them into pieces about ¼ inch thick and 3 to 4 inches in diameter. Pour vegetable oil into a small deep skillet or saucepan to a depth of about 1 inch. When the oil is hot (about 375°F), fry one or two pieces of dough at a time, turning once, until each side is golden brown and the pizza is puffed, about 1 minute on each side. Remove from the pan with a slotted spoon to a plate lined with paper towels. Serve the pizza fritte warm.

Chapter 12

DESSERT PIZZA

few years ago I was asked by a small pizza company in San Francisco to come up with some ideas for sweet pizzas. I tinkered and toiled for several weeks and came up with quite an assortment of sweet or dessert pizzas. Sweet pizzas are wonderful on a brunch buffet or as a tasty ending to a simple luncheon or dinner. Even nicer is the fact that many of these sweet pies can be served hot from the oven or slightly chilled. Conveniently, the various components that make up a sweet pizza can be prepared ahead, with the final assembly and baking taking less than 30 minutes.

One of the more interesting aspects of sweet pizzas is that the flavor can be varied by the choice of fruit jam or preserves used.

BANANA AND PB PIZZA

A sweet pizza that's a big hit with children—to make and to eat. The caramel sauce is most delicious and a snap to make.

Makes one 12-inch pizza

> 1 recipe Sweet Pizza Dough (page 31)
> 2 tablespoons strawberry jam, heated or microwaved to a spreadable consistency
> 3 rounded tablespoons creamy peanut butter, heated or microwaved to a spreadable consistency
> 3 (about ¾ pound) bananas, peeled and sliced crosswise ½ inch thick
> ¼ cup Caramel Sauce, homemade (recipe follows) or store-bought

With your fingers, press and form (or braid) a 1-inch border around the crust.

Brush the crust, including the border, with the jam. Spread the peanut butter evenly over the crust up to the border. Arrange the bananas evenly over the peanut butter. Drizzle the caramel sauce over the bananas.

Bake the pizza on the bottom rack of a preheated 450°F oven for 10–12 minutes or until the crust is golden brown. Let cool for 5 minutes before cutting and serving.

OPTIONS
Sprinkle chopped nuts over the pizza after it comes out of the oven.

CARAMEL SAUCE

½ cup packed light brown sugar

¼ cup light corn syrup

¼ cup whipping cream or half-and-half

2 tablespoons unsalted butter

Combine all the ingredients in a saucepan and cook over low heat until the mixture boils. Let simmer gently for 3 minutes (keep an eye on the heat so it doesn't boil over). Refrigerate for 20 minutes before using. The sauce keeps in the refrigerator, covered, for several weeks. It thickens when chilled, so you may need to heat it or leave it at room temperature for about 1 hour before using.

ESPRESSO SYRUP

¾ cup firmly packed light brown sugar

2 tablespoons light corn syrup

¼ cup water

1 tablespoon instant espresso powder ⭑

1 teaspoon grated lemon zest

2 teaspoons unsalted butter

Combine the sugar, corn syrup, and water in a saucepan and bring to a slow boil, stirring, until the sugar is dissolved. Whisk in the coffee powder and lemon zest. Simmer for 3 minutes. Whisk in the butter.

Let the syrup cool in the refrigerator for 20 minutes before using. The syrup will keep in the refrigerator, in a sealed jar, for several months. The sauce thickens when chilled, so you may need to heat it or leave it at room temperature for about 1 hour before using.

⭑ Instant espresso powder is available at Italian food markets and specialty food stores.

SWEET RICOTTA PIE WITH ESPRESSO SYRUP

This sweet pizza is a cross between tiramisu and a cannoli filling. You will have more espresso syrup than you will need, but it is addictive, so don't hold back.

Makes one 12-inch pizza

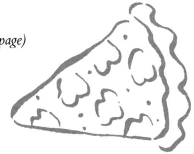

1 recipe Sweet Pizza Dough (page 31)
5 tablespoons Espresso Syrup (recipe on previous page)
1 cup ricotta cheese, drained of excess water
½ cup confectioners' sugar
½ teaspoon grated lemon zest
1 large egg, lightly beaten
¼ cup miniature chocolate chips
2 teaspoons unsweetened cocoa powder

With your fingers, press and form (or braid) a 1-inch border around the crust.

Brush the crust and border with 3 tablespoons of the cooled but not chilled Espresso Syrup. Set aside.

In a mixing bowl or food processor, whip the ricotta and sugar to a smooth, spreadable consistency. Beat in the lemon zest and the egg. Fold in the chocolate chips. (The ricotta mixture can be made several hours ahead and refrigerated.)

Spread the ricotta mixture evenly over the crust up to the border, smoothing the top.

Using the tines of a fork, drizzle about 2 tablespoons of the Espresso Syrup over the cheese filling.

Bake the pizza on the bottom rack of a preheated 425°F oven for 18–20 minutes or until the cheese is set and the crust turns a deep amber brown.

Chill the pizza, covered, for 1 hour or overnight before serving. Just before serving, dust the top evenly and liberally with the cocoa powder.

PEACHES 'N' CREAM PIZZA

Rich and silky mascarpone cheese, sweet ripe peaches, an amaretti cookie streusel . . . I really enjoy making and serving this sweet pizza, because it puts a wide smile on the face of my guests. The streusel can be made ahead, and so can the mascarpone filling. The pizza tastes even better when refrigerated for 24 hours.

Makes one 12-inch pizza

> ½ pound mascarpone cheese
> ¼ cup confectioner's sugar
> 1 teaspoon grated lemon zest
> 1 teaspoon amaretto liqueur
> 1 recipe Sweet Pizza Dough (page 31)
> 2 tablespoons strawberry jam, heated or microwaved to liquefy
> 4 dead-ripe peaches, peeled, stoned, and halved, or 8 canned freestone
>   peach halves, drained
> 1 recipe Amaretti Cookie Streusel (recipe follows)

In a small mixing bowl, combine the mascarpone, sugar, lemon zest, and amaretto and beat with a large spoon until smooth.

With your fingers, press and form a ½-inch border (or braid) around the crust.

With a pastry brush, brush the crust and crust border with the jam. Spread the mascarpone mixture evenly over the crust up to the border. Arrange the peaches, cut side down, evenly over the pizza, pushing them gently into the mascarpone. Sprinkle all of the streusel over the pizza.

Bake the pizza in a preheated 450°F oven for 12–14 minutes or until the streusel crisps and turns dark brown. Slip the pizza onto a wire rack and let cool for 1 hour. Put the pizza on a large plate or clean pizza pan and cool, covered, in the refrigerator for at least 2 hours or overnight before serving.

AMARETTI COOKIE STREUSEL

Makes topping for one 12-inch pizza

  ¼ cup unbleached all-purpose flour

  ¼ cup packed light brown sugar

  ¼ teaspoon ground cinnamon

  1 tablespoon granulated sugar

  3 tablespoons unsalted butter, cut into small pieces

  2 ounces Amaretti cookie crumbs, ground in a food processor or blender (about ½ cup)

In small mixing bowl, combine the flour, light brown sugar, cinnamon, and granulated sugar. Work the bits of butter into the mixture with your fingers to form a coarse crumble. Add the ground Amaretti cookies and combine thoroughly. The streusel can be made several days ahead and refrigerated, tightly covered.

Pizza Trivia

Pizzaioli is the Italian word for "pizza-maker." It is as much a compliment to use this word as it is to call an expert cook a chef.

APPLE PIZZA PIE

Makes one 14-inch pizza

STREUSEL TOPPING

½ cup unbleached all-purpose flour

½ cup packed light brown sugar

½ teaspoon ground cinnamon

2 tablespoons granulated sugar

4 tablespoons unsalted butter, cut into bits

In a small mixing bowl, combine the flour, brown sugar, cinnamon, and granulated sugar. Mix the butter in with your fingertips to form small crumbles. You will have 1½ cups of streusel. Set aside.

THE REST

3–4 large Granny Smith apples (about 2½ pounds), peeled, cored, and
cut into ¼-inch slices

1 tablespoon fresh lemon juice

2 tablespoons unsalted butter

2 tablespoons light brown sugar

1 teaspoon ground cinnamon

3 tablespoons apricot jam or preserves

1 recipe Basic Pizza Dough II (page 25)

In a mixing bowl, toss the apple slices with the lemon juice.

In a sauté pan over high heat, melt the butter until it just begins to froth. Add the apple slices and cook, stirring occasionally, for 4 minutes. Add the brown sugar and cinnamon and cook for 2 minutes or until the apples are barely tender. Transfer the apples to a bowl and let cool for 10 minutes.

In a small saucepan, cook the apricot jam until it liquefies. Set aside.

With your fingers, press and form a ½-inch border around the crust.

Brush the entire top of the crust, including the border, with the apricot jam.

Spread the reserved apples evenly over the crust. Sprinkle the streusel over the apples.

Bake the pizza in a preheated 450°F oven for 15 minutes. Let the pizza sit for 10 minutes before cutting and serving.

OPTIONS

♦ Sprinkle ½ cup chopped walnuts over the streusel.

♦ Sprinkle ½ cup grated cheddar over the streusel before baking.

Pizza Trivia

Alexandre Dumas, author of *The Three Musketeers,* wrote pizza trivia in a series of travel essays. "At first glance it seems to be simple," he said, "but on closer inspection it is seen to be really complicated. Pizza is made with oil, pork fat, lard, cheese, tomato or small fish. Pizza is the yardstick by which the food market is priced; prices rise and fall according to the prices of its ingredients and their availability."

In Calabria, pizza (*pitta* in Calabrian dialect) dough gets a tablespoon or two of *strutto,* or pork fat, which confirms Mr. Dumas's description of how pizza was made in the southern part of Italy.

Nearly 2 billion pounds of mozzarella cheese is used annually in the United States.

CREAM CHEESE AND PINEAPPLE PIZZA

Makes one 14-inch pizza

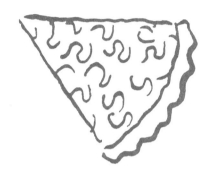

1 recipe Basic Pizza Dough II (page 25)

3 tablespoons strawberry jam

½ pound soft cream cheese

2 tablespoons milk or cream

¼ cup confectioners' sugar

½ teaspoon vanilla extract

8 slices pineapple (rings)

2 tablespoons light brown sugar

With your fingers, press and form a ½-inch border around the crust.

In a small saucepan over low heat, liquefy the jam and spread it over the entire top of the crust including the border.

In a mixing bowl, combine the cream cheese, milk, sugar, and vanilla. Beat with a wooden spoon until smooth.

Spread the cream cheese mixture evenly over the crust up to the border. Arrange the pineapple rings on top of the cream cheese. Sprinkle the light brown sugar evenly over the pizza.

Bake the pizza in a preheated 450°F oven for 15 minutes. Let the pizza sit for 10 minutes before cutting and serving. This pizza is better served at room temperature or cold from the refrigerator.

OPTIONS

Arrange maraschino cherries in and around the pineapple slices.

APPENDIX

A GUIDE TO PIZZA RESTAURANTS AROUND THE WORLD

The long arm of Neapolitan pizza has reached out and wrapped itself around the world. Who would have thought that a humble food, food that was at one time sold by street urchins in the alleys and byways of Naples, would become the most popular food worldwide? In my travels I have enjoyed pizza in many countries. Here are some of my personal recommendations for pizza enjoyment around the world. Buon appetito!

AUSTRALIA

Melbourne

Pinocchio's Pizza, 142 Toorak Rd. (South Yarra)

Sydney

Andiamo, 292 Victoria St. (Darlinghurst)

BRAZIL

Rio de Janeiro

Gatopardo, Av. Borges de Medeiros, 1426 (Lagoa)

ENGLAND

London

Lorelei, 2l Bateman St., W1

Orsino, 119 Portland Rd., W11

Orso, 27 Wellington St., WC2

FRANCE

Nice

Icardo, Rte de Grenoble, 234

Paris

Pizza Pino, 43 Rue St Denis (1er)

Pizzeria Les Artistes, Blvd. de Grenelle, 98 (15th)

Villefranche-sur-Mer

Carpaccio, Promenade des Marinieres

GREECE

Nikos and Maria's King Pizza, Ayia Anna Square, Mykonos

HONG KONG

Marco Polo Pizza, 23 Lan Kwai Fong (Central)

Numero Uno, 1 Village Rd. (Happy Valley)

The Pizzeria, Kowloon Hotel (2nd floor), 19–21 Nathan Rd. (Tsim Sha Tsui)

Tivoli, 130 Austin Rd. (Tsim Sha Tsui)

ITALY

Amalfi

The Green Bar, Via Pietro Capuano

Assisi (Umbria)

Da Otello, Piazzetta Chiesa Nuova

Bergamo (Lombardy)

Valletta, Via Castagneta, 19

Ristorante-Pizzeria San Vigilio, Via S. Vigilio, 34

Cortina d'Ampezzo (Veneto)

De la Poste Hotel Ristorante, Piazza Roma, 14

Ferrara (Emilia–Romagna)

Piper, Corso Porto Reno, 22

Florence (Tuscany)

Borgo Antico, Piazza Santo Spirito, 4

Forno Sartoni, Via dei Cerchi, 34

Il Forno Galli, Via Matteo Palmieri, 24

Pizzeria Marchetti, Via Calzaiuoli, 109

Pizzeria Nutti, Borgo San Lorenzo

Genoa (Liguria)

Da Guglie, Via San Vincenzo, 64

Ischia

'O Padrone d'O Mare, Lacco Ameno

Lecce (Apulia)

Tarocchi, Via Idomeneo

Milan (Lombardy)

di Gennaro, Via S. Radegonda, 14

Pizzeria da Giulio, Viale Bligny, 29

Pizzeria Il Mozzo, Via Ravizzi, 1

Premiatia Pizzeria, Via Alzaia Naviglio Grande, 2

Vecchia Napoli da Rino, Via Chavez, 4

Naples (Campania)

Antica Pizzeria Port 'Alba (reputedly the oldest pizzeria in Italy), via Port 'Alba, 19

Bellini, Via Santa Maria di Costantinopoli, 80

Da Pasqualino, Piazza Sannazzaro, 78

La Brace, Via Silvio Spaventa, 16

Lombardi di Santa Chiara, Via Benedetto Croce, 59

Pizzeria Condurro (aka Da Michele), Via Cesare Sersale, 1-3

Pizzeria Trianon Da Ciro, Via Pietro Colletta, 46

Palermo (Sicily)

Ristorante/Pizzeria Italia, Via dell'Orologio

Rome (Lazio)

44, Via Flavia, 44

Caffe Barardo, Piazza Colonna

Er Grottini Via dei Baullari, 25/27

Pizza Rustica al Gracchi, Via dei Gracchi

Pizzeria Baffetto, Via del Governo Vecchio, 114 (Piazza Navona)

Pizzeria Panattoni, Viale di Trastevere, 53/59

Pizzeria Remo, Piazza di Santa Maria Liberatrice, 44 (Testaccio)

Salerno

La Rosalia, Via Degli Orti, 22

Tavola Calda da Tavola Calda, Via G. Vicinanza, 7

San Gimignano

Chiribiri, Piazetta Della Madonna, 1

Santa Margherita Ligure (Liguria)

Da Alfonso, Piazza Martiri della Liberta, 47

Sardinia

Costa Smeralda

Il Pomodoro, Port Cervo

Siena

Malborghetto Pizzeria Braceria, Via Porta Giustizia, 6

Taormina

La Botte, Piazza San Domenico

Torino (Piedmont)

Carignano, Piazza Carignano, 7

Trapani (Sicily)

Pizzeria Calvino, Via N. Nasi, 79

Urbino (The Marches)

Pizzeria La Rustica, Via Nuova, 3

Venice (Veneto)

Al Teatro, Campo San Fantin

Alle Oche, San Polo 1552/A, Calle del Tintor

Vicenza (Veneto)

La Taverna, Piazza dei Signori, 47

Pizzeria Vesuvio, Corso Palladio, 24

MALTA

La Ronde Pizzeria, 5 Windmill St., Valletta

MEXICO

Mexico City

Pizzeria Due Due, Centro Commercial K-Mart, San Mateo Av. Adolfo
Lopez Mateos, 201; Insurgentes Sur No. 1798, Colonia Florida

MOROCCO

PizzAmerica, 25, Rue Moulay Ali Cherif, Rabat

ST. BART S

L'Escale, Rue Jeanne d'Arc, Gustavia

SPAIN

Barcelona

Pizza World, Francesc Niragasm 27 (Sant Cugat) (and other locations throughout Spain)

Madrid

TelePizza, C/. Cochabamba, No. 19 (and other locations around Madrid)

UNITED STATES

Arizona

Scottsdale
Cafe Terra Cotta, 6166 N. Scottsdale Rd., The Borgata

Tucson
Cafe Terra Cotta, 4310 N. Campbell Ave., St. Phillips Plaza
Magpie's, 4654 E. Speedway (and other locations)

California

Los Angeles and Vicinity
Angeli, 7274 Melrose
Bistango, 1900 Von Karman Ave., Irvine
Caioti, 2100 Laurel Canyon Blvd., Hollywood
Il Forno, 2901 Ocean Park Blvd.
Osteria Nonni, 3219 Glendale Blvd.
Spago, 1114 Horn Ave.

San Diego
Pizza Nova, 5120 N. Harbor Dr., Point Loma

San Francisco and Vicinity
Cafe Roma, 414 Columbus Ave.
Il Fornaio, 1265 Battery St.
Palio, 640 Sacramento St.
Piemonte, 3909 Grand Ave., Oakland
Tommaso's, 1042 Kearny St.
Tra Vigne, 1050 Charter Oak, St. Helena

Connecticut
Pepe's, 157 Wooster St., New Haven

Florida
Picasso's Pizza, 2275 S. Federal Hwy., Delray Beach

Illinois

Chicago

Bacino's, 75 E. Wacker Dr.

Cafe Luigi, 2458 N. Clark St.

Cafe Spiaggia, 980 N. Michigan Ave.

Carlucci, 2215 N. Halsted St.

Gino's East Pizzeria, 160 E. Superior St.

Home Run Inn, 4254 W. 31st St.

O'Fame, 750 W. Webster St.

Palermo Pizzeria, 3751 W. 63rd St.

Pizzeria Uno, 29 E. Ohio St.

Scoozi, 410 W. Huron St.

Tuttaposto, 646 N. Franklin St.

Vinci, 1732 N. Halsted St.

Freeport

Cannova's, 1101 W. Empire St.

Massachusetts

Boston and Vicinity

Bertucci's, 799 Main St., Cambridge

Caffe Lampara, 916 Commonwealth Ave.

Pizzeria Regina, 11½ Thatcher St. (North End)

Sorrento's Italian Gourmet, 86 Peterborough St.

Minnesota

Minneapolis/St. Paul

Broadway Station, Broadway and W. River Rd., Minneapolis

Cossetta Italian Market, 211 W. 7th St., St. Paul

D'Amico & Sons, 2210 Hennepin Ave. S. and 2727 W. 43rd St., Minneapolis

Missouri

St. Louis

First Federal Frank & Crust Co., 13 Saint Louis Galleria

Rigazzi's, 4945 Daggett

New York

Albany

Mangia Wood-Fired Pizza & Pasta, Stuyvesant Plaza

New York City and Vicinity

Famous Ray's, 465 Ave. of the Americas

Goodfella's Pizza, 1718 Hylan Blvd. (Dongan Hills), Staten Island

John's, 278 Bleecker St., and 408 E. 64th St.

Patsy's, 19 Old Fulton St., Brooklyn

Olean

Napoli Pizza, 683 E. State St.

Rhode Island

Providence

Adesso, 161 Cushing St.

Al Forno, 577 S. Main St.

Caserta Pizzeria, 121 Spruce St.

Texas

Austin

Pizza Nizza, 1608 Barton Springs Rd.

Washington

Seattle

Pizzeria Pagliacci, 4529 University Way

Romio's Pizza, 2001 W. Dravus

TestaRossa, 210 Broadway East

INDEX